MR. CIVIL RIGHTS
The Story of Thurgood Marshall

Notable Americans

MR. CIVIL RIGHTS
The Story of Thurgood Marshall

Nancy Whitelaw

**MORGAN
REYNOLDS**
Incorporated

Greensboro

TB Marshall

MR. CIVIL RIGHTS *The Story of Thurgood Marshall*

Cover photo courtesy of AP/Wide World Photos

Library of Congress Cataloging-in-Publication Data
Whitelaw, Nancy.-
    Mr. Civil Rights : the story of Thurgood Marshall / Nancy Whitelaw. — 1st ed.
        p.   cm. -- (Notable Americans)
    Includes bibliographical references and index.
    Summary: A biography of the civil rights advocate who was the first African American to
be appointed to the Supreme Court.
        ISBN   1-883846-10-2
            1. Marshall, Thurgood, 1908-1993—Juvenile literature.   2. Judges--United States--
Biography--Juvenile literature.   3. United States. Supreme Court--Biography--Juvenile
literature.   4. Civil rights--United States--History--Juvenile literature   [1. Marshall,
Thurgood, 1908-1933. 2. Judges. 3. United States. Supreme Court--Biography. 4. Afro-
Americans--Biography.] I. Title II. Series
KF8745. M34W47   1995
347. 73' 2634—dc20
[B]
[347. 3073534]
[B]
                                                                                95-10481
                                                                                     CIP
                                                                                     AC

Printed in the United States of America
First Edition

This book is dedicated to Pat Broderick:
From my early years as a writer,
you have been a highlight in my life.

Acknowledgements

I am grateful to Joyce Stanton, who gave me the inspiration and courage to write this biography of Justice Thurgood Marshall. She stood close by with help and encouragement throughout the project.

I am also indebted to several generous people who answered my requests for information. They are, in alphabetical order: Joseph Benforado, Louise Jefferson, Bernie Levy, Will Maslow, Margo Miller, Deborah L. Rhode, and James Sweet.

I thank Michael Davis, co-author of *Thurgood Marshall: Warrior at the Bar, Rebel at the Bench*, for reviewing the manuscript.

CONTENTS

Chapter One
"You learn to take it."

Fourteen-year-old Thurgood Marshall could not see where he was going. A delivery boy for an exclusive Baltimore clothing shop, he carried four large hat boxes that blocked his view. As the trolley he was riding clattered to a stop, he blindly judged the distance to the first step and reached out with his right foot.

Suddenly an angry voice yelled, "Nigga, don't you never push in front of no white lady again."

Then a hand grabbed Thurgood's shoulder, forcing him backwards. Thurgood lost his balance and his temper at the same time. He slipped off the step, regained his balance, dropped the boxes, whirled, and punched the white man who had pushed him. When the man lunged toward him, Thurgood hit him in the ribs. In an instant, the two were wrestling.

Passers-by came running. They grabbed the fighters by their sleeves, forced their arms down, and pulled them apart. A police officer yelled, "Break it up! You're under arrest," and seized Thurgood's shoulder.

Thurgood stood still, catching his breath. His fists were bruised, and his whole body hurt. He was afraid his boss would fire him for fighting on the job.

At the police station, both he and the man told their stories, a common tale of racial conflict. His employer, Mr. Schoen, came to the police station and Thurgood apologized to him for the commotion. Mr. Schoen's answer surprised him. "When I saw what you did to the other guy," he said, "I decided it was worth the loss."

Mr. Schoen put up bail for Thurgood. Later, the case was dismissed.

Thurgood's father approved, too. After all, Thurgood was only following his father's directions: "If anybody calls you nigger, you not only got my permission to fight him—you got my orders."

Thurgood Marshall was born in Baltimore, Maryland in 1908. The next year, the Marshalls moved to Harlem, New York. There his mother, Norma Marshall, studied for an advanced degree in teaching at Columbia University. His father, William Marshall, worked as a dining-car waiter on the Baltimore & Ohio Railroad.

The family moved back to Baltimore in 1913 when Thurgood was five years old. Thurgood, his ten-year-old brother Aubrey, and their teacher mother went off to segregated elementary schools each day. Mr. Marshall waited tables at an exclusive whites-only country club.

Thurgood learned to take care of himself early. In the second grade he changed his name from Thoroughgood to Thurgood. "I got tired of spelling all that and shortened it," he explained. He could take care of himself in the neighborhood, too. He described the difference between himself and his brother:

> We lived on a respectable street, but behind us were back
> alleys where roughnecks and the tough kids hung out.
> When it was time for dinner, my mother used to go to the

Thurgood Marshall poses for his high school graduation photo, 1924. (Collection of the Supreme Court of the United States)

front door to call my older brother. Then she'd go to the back door and call me.

Both boys learned to avoid the fights over race they could not win. "The truth is," Thurgood said later, "you learn to take it. I was taught to go along with it, not to fight it unless you could win it. The only thing was if somebody calls you a nigger."

A neighbor described Thurgood as thoughtful: "I can still see him coming down Division Street every Sunday afternoon around one o'clock. He'd be wearing knee pants with both hands dug way into his pockets and be kicking a stone in front of him as he crossed over to Dolphin Street to visit his grandparents at their big grocery store on the corner. He was in a deep study, that boy, and it was plain something was going on inside him."

Mrs. Marshall insisted that both Thurgood and Aubrey do their homework. She wanted them to become professionals: Aubrey, a doctor, and Thurgood a dentist. Mr. Marshall had different plans for his sons. He hoped one of them would be a lawyer. In his free time, he would sit in the courthouse with Thurgood at his side. They watched white lawyers and white judges argue cases in which the defendants were African American. Mr. Marshall often discussed court cases over the dinner table. He told his family that one day discrimination would be outlawed. The United States Constitution promised that, he said, and he had faith in the Constitution.

Sometimes, Mr. Marshall treated Thurgood and Aubrey as though they were defendants in court. He insisted they give logical explanations for what they said. Thurgood said, "He never told me to become a lawyer, but he turned me into one ... He taught me how to argue, challenged my logic on every point...even if we... were discussing the weather." Thurgood told an interviewer later, "My dad, my brother, and I had the most violent arguments you ever heard about anything. I guess we argued five out of seven nights at the dinner table."

At least one other family member had ideas about Thurgood's future. His grandmother, who lived with the family, taught him to cook. "I am with your parents in wanting you to be a professional man," she said, "but I want to make sure you can always earn a dollar. You can pick up all that other stuff later, but I bet you never saw a jobless Negro cook." Thurgood enjoyed cooking. Baltimore was famous for soft-shell crabs, and he learned to make a popular crab soup.

But always there was the issue of race. Most African American youngsters in Baltimore, Maryland—and in much of the rest of the United States—were treated as though they were not as good as whites. They were allowed to use only the public restrooms labeled "colored." They had to pay at the front door of the bus and then go to the back door to enter. Books and gym equipment at their schools were usually old and worn-down. Few African Americans dared to complain—policemen were quick to arrest any black who seemed to be making trouble. Because policemen, lawyers, and judges were white, an African American did not have a chance.

Thurgood never forgot a humiliating incident in downtown Baltimore. He needed a restroom, but none were open to him. Although he raced home, he did not get there in time to take care of himself.

The racial stigma even extended into the black community. Many blacks believed that lighter skin was "better" than darker skin. Both

William and Norma were mulattos, of mixed white and African American ancestry, and both of their sons were light-skinned. But the Marshalls refused to take part in this black-against-black prejudice.

Despite the oppression, Thurgood loved the social life of high school. He joined clubs, played on teams, and went to dances and parties. He kept his grades up so he could become a dentist as his mother wanted.

Thurgood paid less attention to discipline than to his studies. He often provoked his teachers until they sent him out of the classroom and into the basement. He was ordered to stay there until he had memorized passages from the Constitution. Thurgood spent hours learning phrases like:

equal protection of the laws

speedy and public trial

impartial jury

cruel and unusual punishments

right of citizens of the United States to vote.

"Before I left that school, "Thurgood said, "I knew the entire Constitution by heart."

The location of the school created unforgettable memories. Douglass High was next door to a police station. On warm days when the windows were open, Thurgood sometimes could hear police beating prisoners.

By his senior year of high school, Thurgood was eager for college. He enjoyed Aubrey's stories of college life, and knew that he could succeed, too. Some of his confidence came from his success in high school, some came from hearing stories about his family. Thurgood was born less than fifty years after the Civil War, and many of his ancestors had been slaves. His maternal great grandfather was brought from the Congo to America by slave traders in the 1840s. Thurgood loved to tell the story about this slave whom he called "one mean man":

> His more polite descendants like to think he came from the cultured tribes in Sierra Leone, but we all know that he really came from the toughest part of the Congo. One day his owner came up to him and said, "Look, I brought you here so I guess I can't very well shoot you—as you deserve. On the other hand, I can't with a clear conscience sell anyone as vicious as you to another slaveholder, and I can't give you away. So, I am going to set you free—on one condition. Get the hell out of this county and never come back." That was the only time Massuh didn't get an argument from the old boy. He was a real no good, and his master was right.

Thurgood's paternal grandfather, Marshall, was born a slave. Like many slaves, he had only one name—the name of his owner. When he was freed, Marshall joined an African American unit of the Union army. When he became a soldier for the North, the enlistment officer asked him to sign two names. Marshall quickly chose a second name that made him sound like a fine person. The name was Thoroughgood. Thoroughgood married Annie who was also a free person. According to one story, Annie objected when the electric company wanted to put a light pole on the sidewalk in front of Grandpa Marshall's grocery store. She said that the sidewalk belonged to her and her husband. For weeks, she sat in a kitchen chair on the spot designated for the pole. Eventually officials of the electric company gave up. Thurgood said later, "Finally Grandma Annie emerged as the victor of what may have been the first successful sitdown strike in Maryland."

Another family member who inspired Thurgood was Isaiah Olive Branch Williams, his maternal grandfather. In the 1870s, Williams organized demonstrations to protest police brutality against African Americans.

Discrimination narrowed the Marshalls' lives, but it did not make them inferior. They were proud of each other, of their Congo ancestors, of Thoroughgood and Annie Marshall, of Isaiah Williams, and of the millions of others who shared their racial background. From a young age, Thurgood felt the responsibility of living up to the legendary deeds of his ancestors.

When he was a high school student, Thurgood decided to go to Lincoln University, an African American college in Pennsylvania. Tuition, room, and board would cost $300 a year, more than the Marshall family could afford. Thurgood started saving. He worked as delivery boy for a hat shop. He also waited on tables in the dining cars of the B&O Railroad as his father had.

On his first working day on the railroad, his employer gave him a pair of waiter's pants. Thurgood was over six feet tall. The waiter who wore them before Thurgood was much shorter. Thurgood told his employer the pants didn't fit.

"Boy," his boss answered, "we can get a man to fit the pants a lot easier than we can get pants to fit the man. Why don't you scrunch down a little more?"

Thurgood did not argue. He "scrunched."

Thurgood married Vivian "Buster" Burey" in 1929. (Howard University)

His mother pawned her engagement ring to help make the first payments on college bills. In September 1925, seventeen-year-old Thurgood entered Lincoln University.

Chapter Two
"That's what started the whole thing."

At Lincoln, Thurgood made lots of friends fast. Talking and playing cards were two of his favorite pastimes. He was so good at the card game pinochle that he picked up most of his spending money by gambling.

With friends, Thurgood frequently went to night clubs, theaters, and restaurants in Philadelphia. He started the Weekend Club, whose members boasted that they never studied on weekends, and the handsome six-foot-two student seemed to have no trouble attracting coeds. "At one point," he boasted, "I had six fraternity rings out at the same time."

College was fun but there was always the need for money. Thurgood worked in the school bakery, kneading bread and mixing pies and cakes, using skills his grandmother taught him. Every night after work, he took a loaf of hot bread, slit it open and filled it with butter—the perfect late-night snack.

Because of his court-room style discussions with his father, Thurgood had a head start as a debater. For school debates, he spent long hours preparing speeches, always careful to back up his statements with plenty of facts. He wrote to his parents: "If I were taking debating for credit, I would be the biggest honor student they ever had around here." Some members of his debating team called him "Wrathful" Marshall. They claimed he frightened his opponents right from the beginning of each debate with his height, his heavy build, and his determined expression.

Sophomores at Lincoln, as at many colleges, enjoyed hazing freshmen. When Thurgood was a sophomore, he and his friends had what they thought was a great idea. They shaved the freshmen's heads. The school administration failed to see the humor of their actions. They fined the group $125, and suspended Thurgood and the other ringleaders for two weeks. The boys took advantage of the suspension. They went to New York with plans to get jobs on a ship traveling around the world. But nobody would hire them. They returned to Lincoln and became students again.

Thurgood later explained why he became a protest leader in some "mini-strikes:"

> .... you had to do something to let out your steam. So when spring would come around we would find some reason ... [like] the food in the dining room. That's always bad, so it was always a good reason. And we would stay out of school and walk around and picket and things like that, and after a reasonable time, we'd find some ground where we could save face and the school could save face, and we'd go back.

One afternoon, Thurgood and a group of students decided to integrate a local movie theater. Six fellows drove downtown in a Model T car. When they bought their tickets, the ticket seller reminded them that they would have to sit in the balcony, commonly called "nigger heaven."

They asked why.

The seller said she didn't know why, but she knew they had to sit there.

The students entered the theater. They saw a few white patrons seated in the downstairs section. They marched past them and took seats close to the front, a few rows away from the whites.

They were watching the Western movie when an usher approached them.

"You can't sit here," he said.

None of the students seemed to hear him. They kept their eyes on the cowboys riding across the screen.

The usher spoke louder, "You can't sit here."

The students didn't move.

Thurgood heard a voice behind him. "Nigger, why don't you-all just get out of here and go sit where you belong?"

He whirled around. He fought his instinct to hit the man for calling him a nigger. Instead he said he had paid for his ticket and intended to sit where he wanted.

The man left the theater. The students watched the rest of the movie undisturbed.

Thurgood wrote to his father:

> We found out that they only had one fat cop in the whole town, and they wouldn't have had the nerve or the room in the jail to arrest all of us. But the amazing thing was, when we were leaving we just walked out with all those other people and they didn't do anything, didn't say a thing, didn't even look at us—at least, as far as I know. I'm not

sure I like being invisible, but maybe it's better than being put to shame and not able to respect yourself."

After that night, Lincoln students sat anywhere they wished in the movie theater. Remembering the incident years later, Thurgood said: "I guess that's what started the whole thing in my life."

Thurgood began to realize he did not want to become a dentist. Later, he said, "At times I think I'm sorry .... Then I tell myself I'm glad. Hell, my hands are too big to put in somebody's mouth."

Thurgood believed that he could succeed as a professional. Others had broken the color barrier to become specialists in their fields, such as singer Paul Robeson, writers Carter Woodson and W.E.B. DuBois, and marine biologist Ernest Just. In addition, many personal experiences made law particularly interesting to him—memorizing the Constitution in the cellar of the high school, watching court sessions with his father, arguing at the family dinner table, participating in debates, challenging discrimination in the theater near Lincoln.

During his junior year, Thurgood often attended services at a Baptist church in Philadelphia with his friends. "We went there because we learned that's where all the cute chicks met," Thurgood explained. There he met Vivian "Buster" Burey, a student at the University of Pennsylvania. He described her, "black hair, black eyes, and *very nice.*"

Buster said it was definitely not love at first sight for her. She told Thurgood, "you were so busy arguing with everybody else at the table that you didn't pay any attention to me."

Whatever the beginning of the courtship, the two twenty-year-old students were soon deeply in love. Thurgood's mother objected to their plans to marry. They were too young and too poor, she said.

Thurgood used his strongest debate techniques with his mother. He argued that he could study more if he did not spend time traveling forty miles each way from Oxford to Philadelphia to see Buster. Furthermore, he had already proven that he was responsible. During the school year he worked two jobs, one as a grocery clerk and the other as a baker. During the summers, he worked full-time as waiter on the railroad. Surely he had proved he could handle finances.

The debater won. Thurgood and Buster were married in 1929, the beginning of Thurgood's senior year. Buster dropped out of the college to take a job as secretary.

Thurgood loved to tell a story about working as a waiter in the same country club as his father. Thurgood's father overheard one patron, a United States senator, calling Thurgood "nigger." He thundered at his son: "Thurgood, you are a disgrace to the colored people!"

Later, in the soft Southern dialect he often used to tell stories, Thurgood explained his attitude toward the senator:

> "Hey, Nigger," [the Senator] yells over. Now I hear what he say, and I didn't like the idea of his callin' me that, not one bit. But ah go on over anyway, and he says, "Nigger, I want service at this table!" So ah give him the service an' he is always callin' me nigger all during the meal an' ah'm likin' it less and less. But when he gets up to go, he leaves me a twenty-dollah tip. Now this crude fella keeps comin' into the club and keeps on callin' me nigger—keeps on leavin' me twenty-dollah tips. In a few days, I got myself almost enough money to pay off all my bills.

Later when he told this story, Thurgood added that he told the senator: "Any time you wanna call me 'nigger,' you just put your twenty dollars down on this table. And you can keep doing it all day. But the second you run outta them twenties, I'm gonna bust you in the nose."

Near the end of his senior year, Thurgood wanted to apply to the University of Maryland Law School. UM was an excellent school only 10 minutes away from his home, and tuition for in-state residents was reasonable. But he could not get in. African Americans were not admitted to the school. Instead he enrolled at Howard University Law School in Washington, D.C., a widely respected school for African Americans. Thurgood knew he was lucky to be attending any law school. The Great Depression had struck and jobs were hard to get in 1930. Buster finally landed a secretarial position in Baltimore. To save money, the couple moved in with Thurgood's parents.

Howard University Law School did not look much like a college. Classes and offices were located in a three-story building that was formerly a family residence. The building was one in a series of row houses in a black neighborhood. The "lecture hall" was a vestibule furnished with wooden benches.

Thurgood got up at 5:00 every morning to catch the train from Baltimore. He took a seat in the blacks-only car for the forty-minute trip. He learned to appreciate commuting since he could study all the way to school and back.

After just one week at Howard, he said, "This is what I wanted to do for as long as I lived." Many afternoons he wished he could study longer, but he had to catch the 3:00 train back to Baltimore. Each day he went to one of his three part-time jobs, as waiter, bellhop, or baker.

One of Thurgood's favorite teachers was Charles Houston, a Harvard graduate and dean of the law school. Thurgood said of him:

> What Charlie beat into our heads was excellence. Houston told his students, "when you get into a courtroom, you can't just say, 'Please, Mr. Court, have mercy on me because I'm a Negro.' You are in competition with a well-trained white lawyer, and you better be at least as good as he is; and if you expect to win, you better be better. If I give you five cases to read overnight, you better read eight."

Hard work didn't bother Thurgood. "When I was in law school in my first year," he said, "I lost 30 pounds solely from work, intellectual work, studying. And that's how you get ahead of people." By June, he was the top student in his class. This earned him the privilege of working in the law library. Now he no longer had to rush to meet the 3:00 train. Instead he spent afternoons with the books that he loved. Best of all, he spent time with Professor Houston in the library, discussing the professor's current cases and working on research with him.

The two men often discussed a U. S. Supreme Court decision of 1896 called *Plessy v Ferguson*, when the judges ruled that whites could be separated from blacks in schools and other public facilities if blacks had school and public facilities of equal quality. This decision established the so-called separate but equal rule.

The separate provision established by *Plessy v Ferguson* required no change in law or custom in much of America, especially across the states of the former Confederacy. But enactment of the equal provision would be expensive, and require sweeping social changes.

When black lawyers went to court and demanded equal treatment, white lawyers and judges answered that government officials needed more time and money.

A generation after the *Plessy v Ferguson* decision, public services were separate—but definitely not equal.

Here are some examples of expenditures for white and black schools: In Missouri, the school board spent $1,000,000 for an athletic field for a white school. The same board spent $30,000 to convert a factory into an African American elementary school. In South Carolina, a white school hired 12 teachers for 276 pupils; an African American school hired 12 teachers for 808 pupils. In Maryland, the average annual pay for a white teacher was $1475; for an African American teacher, it was $612.

When Thurgood was in his second year of law school, Professor William Hastie requested his help on a court case. Professor Hastie was representing Thomas Hocutt in a suit against the University of North Carolina. Hastie planned to base his case upon the 14th Amendment, one of the most important constitutional changes to occur after the Civil War. The 14th Amendment states, in part, that:

> "No State shall make or enforce any law which shall abridge the privileges or immunities of citizens of the United States; nor shall any State deprive any person of life, liberty or property, without due process of law; nor deny to any person within its jurisdiction the equal protection of the laws."

Hastie argued that the 14th Amendment barred state colleges from denying admission to Hocutt on the grounds of race. Hastie lost the

A North Carolina restaurant segregates customers. (Library of Congress)

case named *Hocutt v The University of North Carolina*. But the case helped change the way civil rights lawyers attacked racial injustice. In the future, more civil rights cases would be based upon the 14th Amendment.

Thurgood was disappointed, but not surprised, when the court decided to uphold segregation. He knew the fight for legal equality would take a long time and be filled with disappointments. The case only strengthened his determination to fight injustice.

In one class, professors and students used role-playing to prepare for court cases. The professors took the parts of judges and juries in mock trials. They "held court" for students who took the parts of lawyers.

In another class, Thurgood studied the history of the civil rights movement. He pored through the *Congressional Record*, which recorded everything said in Congress. He found debates on civil rights as far back as 1865, when Southern state legislators passed "Black Code" laws at the same time the U.S. Congress debated the 13th Amendment which outlawed slavery. He became convinced the leaders of the defeated Confederacy had been able to continue slavery by merely changing a few rules.

Thurgood also studied the history of the Ku Klux Klan, an organization of white men created in 1866. The Klan was a secret terrorist group, determined to stop former slaves from enjoying the rights and privileges of American citizenship. The Klan used harassment and humiliation, torture, shooting, burning of people and property, and lynching to achieve its goals. In some areas, Klan members "policed" neighborhoods, warning African Americans to stay in their place. They burned crosses as a symbol of their power. Klan organizations sprang up throughout the country.

While working in the library Thurgood met civil rights lawyers and other activists, including members of the National Association for the Advancement of Colored People (NAACP), an organization founded in 1909 to fight against increasing racial injustice.

Sometimes NAACP members invited Thurgood to their legal discussions. He took part eagerly, and soon became deeply involved in fighting segregation. He and classmates reviewed the District of Columbia law code "just for fun," he said, and were shocked to discover that the code prohibited African Americans from voting. They immediately organized a movement to change the code. The movement was a success.

In 1933, twenty-four-year old Thurgood earned a Bachelor of Laws degree, magna cum laude, with high honors. He was the top student in the class. He passed the Maryland bar exam that same year. Now the young lawyer was prepared to fight to change his country.

Chapter Three
"We're in the education business!"

Harvard Law School offered Thurgood a fellowship. They would give him living expenses if he wanted to study for a doctor of jurisprudence degree. Thurgood turned down the offer. He had been going to school for 20 years. Now he wanted to get out in the world and use the knowledge and skills he had learned.

Eager to begin work, he rented a small office near downtown Baltimore. His mother gave him a prized Oriental rug from her living room, and he bought some second-hand office furniture. Attorney Marshall was ready for business!

However, clients did not come rushing to his office door. Most African Americans assumed they would be better off with a white lawyer in a system where most judges, lawyers, and juries were all-white. A popular saying was: "If you want to go to jail, go to a black lawyer." The Great Depression added to his difficulties. Lawyer's fees were a luxury few could afford. Marshall spent most of his time on minor cases such as traffic infractions, eviction cases, petty theft, and wills and deeds. He became known as the "little man's lawyer," and he often took cases for clients who could not pay. He called it, "justice on a shoestring."

"I bought some fancy stationery that made me look like a hugely successful lawyer when I didn't have a damn dollar to pay for it," Thurgood remembered later. After he was world famous he loved to tell this story from those early years:

> The phone company would call up and say they were going to disconnect my phone. I would bluff and say, "You gonna disconnect *my* phone? Do you realize I'm a lawyer? You mess up with my phone and I'll sue you until *you* pay *me* ... as a matter of fact, you call me one more time and I'm going to rip this phone off the wall and throw it out the goddamn window." And they'd say, "It's all right, Mr. Marshall, it's all right."

In the first year, Marshall spent about $1000 more in expenses than he made in wages.

On the plus side, Marshall had friends all over the city. He became known for his dramatic story-telling and the way he ended each story by slapping his knees and roaring with laughter. He learned to use the term "nigger" in his stories without feeling the hostility which it formerly aroused in him. One of his favorite tales was about a slave who stole and ate his master's turkey. Before the master could whip him, the slave begged, "You shouldn't beat me, massuh. You got less turkey, but you sure got more nigger."

Marshall wanted to build membership in the Baltimore branch of the NAACP. He sometimes had a difficult time recruiting members because of his looks. He was light-skinned, well-dressed, handsome, and confident—much like the whites who controlled the lives of these potential members. He learned to approach people slowly, building friendship and trust before he asked people to join.

He could switch easily from legal language to the language of the streets. In informal groups, he dropped the final *g* sound from words ending in *-ing* (runnin', talkin') and substituted *d* for beginning *th* sounds (dese, dose, dat). His sentences flowed easily into the rhythm he had learned as a child in Baltimore. "It was all part of his strategy," said a NAACP friend. "He never wanted [another black] to think, 'Now this here nigger thinks he's smarter than I am.'"

He encouraged NAACP members to organize a boycott of Baltimore stores. They demonstrated in front of stores which would not hire African Americans for full time work. Store managers sued the NAACP for interfering with their businesses. The case, *A&P Sanitary Stores v Baltimore Branch, NAACP*, went to court. Judges ruled that members of the NAACP had the right to demonstrate.

Marshall took on more civil rights cases for the NAACP. The cases involved police brutality, segregated golf courses, unequal pay for African American teachers, and other discriminations. In 1935, he became a part-time legal counsel for the Baltimore NAACP.

Marshall could not resist accepting civil rights cases, especially when he thought he might win. Between 1935 and 1938, he traveled to nearly all of the twenty-three counties in Maryland. He sued school boards on behalf of African American teachers who earned half as much as white teachers. A few boards yielded to him without a trial; most boards resisted. In Norfolk, Virginia, for example, a superintendent said, "I will not be a party to paying a nigger the same money I pay a white person."

Some white school board members threatened to fire black teachers who organized. Marshall encouraged the teachers to persist in spite of the threats. He won equal-pay agreements with nine county

Attorney Marshall talks with his client Donald Murray, 1935. (Library of Congress)

school boards. In 1939, he persuaded a federal court judge to declare that unequal salaries for public school teachers violated the Constitution.

As NAACP legal counsel, Marshall also worked against discrimination at the college level. In 1935, he and Houston worked on a case for African American Donald Murray who sued the University of Maryland Law School because they rejected his application. In *Murray v the University of Maryland*, a Baltimore court ruled that Murray could not be rejected because of his color.

Outside the courtroom, Marshall celebrated, waving his arms and tapping his feet in a victory dance. "We're in the education business!" he shouted. He said later, referring to his own barring from the UM Law School, "It was sweet revenge, and I enjoyed it no end."

In a case not related to education, Marshall defended a man charged with robbery and murder. Marshall was unable to convince the jury that the defendant was innocent. His client was sentenced to death by hanging. Marshall said, "When the time of execution came up, I felt so bad about it—that maybe I was responsible—that I decided I was going to go and see the execution." When he told a reporter that he was going, the reporter said, "I have been to about a dozen executions, and I have puked at every one of them." The young lawyer decided not to attend, but his opposition to the death penalty was now stronger than ever.

Marshall continued to accept cases whether or not clients could pay his fee. He said that civil rights, not money, was the reason he was in business. "Personally, I would not give up these cases here in Maryland for anything in the world." He added, "But at the same time there is no opportunity to get down to really hustling for business."

About that time, Marshall picked up a nickname that stayed with him the rest of his life. More and more frequently, Thurgood's friends called him "Turkey" because of the way he walked with his head held high and with a kind of strut. He accepted the nickname with good humor. When asked about it, he said he didn't particularly care what people thought about the way he looked.

Marshall was a popular speaker. A reporter wrote:

Thurgood Marshall was *of* the people. He knew how to get through to them. Out in Texas or Oklahoma or down the street here in Washington at the Baptist church, he would make these rousing speeches that would have 'em all jumping out of their seats. He'd explain what he was up to with his law cases in language they could all understand. "We ain't gettin' what we should" was what it came down to, and he made them see that. That was his secret. He knew how to deal with commoners and kings with equal effectiveness.

In 1936, Thurgood sued the Baltimore County Board of Education on behalf of an African American youngster who wanted to attend the school nearest to her home. The case was called *Seventh grade student v Baltimore County Board of Education*. The Maryland court ruled that the school had a right to reject the student because she was black.

That defeat challenged Marshall to keep trying. More and more frequently, he turned down private cases in favor of civil rights cases.

In 1936, Marshall became assistant special counsel for the NAACP in New York City. When Thurgood heard that he would earn $2400 a year, "I whooped and hollered so loud that Buster ran in to see if I was dying."

He laughed about his first trip to national NAACP headquarters in New York in 1936. "How very tush-tush ... It was Dr. Whosis and Mr. Whatsis and all kinds of nonsense like that, bowing and scraping ...Believe me, I had 'em talking first names in nothin' time ... I was gonna relax and operate in my natural-born way ..."

He and Buster rented an apartment in Harlem, New York, where about half a million African Americans lived. The Marshalls enjoyed an exciting social life. Music was a special pleasure, particularly the jazz of Duke Ellington, Roy Minton, and Dinah Washington. They often ate at restaurants, choosing Southern specialties like chitterlings (boiled swine intestines) and spare ribs, and Northern treats like waffles and champagne. Buster was a founding member of the Girl Friends, a social club that spread nationwide.

In their work as counsels for the NAACP, Marshall and his former professor Charles Houston traveled throughout the South. In most places, they were not allowed to stay in the decent hotels. As they traveled, the lawyers met sympathetic residents who welcomed them into their homes. They learned to use their car as an office. Marshall explained, "Charlie would sit in my car—I had a little old beat-up '29 Ford—and type out the briefs."

In 1938, Marshall became chief counsel for the NAACP in New York. The new position brought a raise of $200 a year. He liked to tell a story about the raise:

> When I came home to tell my wife, I was very carried away with the raise. And she said, "Two hundred dollars?" I said,

New attorney Thurgood Marshall poses in his law office in Baltimore.
(Library of Congress)

Yes." She said, "Not that I don't appreciate it, but how much is that a week?"

Marshall plunged into a heavy workload which involved discrimination in travel accommodations, labor contracts, and housing. He won most of the cases.

Despite Thurgood's legal victories, intimidation against African Americans was on the rise. Whites were increasingly uneasy as more blacks demanded equal rights. Segregationist organizations like the Klan grew stronger.

The Texas branch of the NAACP called Marshall to Dallas when a racial incident threatened city-wide violence. Court officers had summoned a man to jury duty, not realizing that he was African American. When they saw his color, they dismissed him. The man, a president of a junior college, insisted that he had a right and a responsibility to serve on a jury. Court employees objected. They dragged him out of the courthouse and down the steps to the sidewalk. The man complained to the NAACP.

Marshall met with Texas governor James Aldred to insist that African Americans be allowed to participate on juries. Immediately after their meeting, Aldred issued a statement: "From now on, not only will citizens be called on for jury duty in Texas regardless of their color, but I'll see to it that Texas Rangers help protect the Negroes who serve." This was a stunning victory for civil rights— and Marshall achieved it without writing a brief or entering a courtroom. Marshall later learned what happened before he arrived in Texas for that meeting with Aldred:

The chief of police told his men a nigger lawyer named Marshall was coming from New York City to cause trouble in town. He told his men he would personally kick the **** out of me ... I sort of considered the idea of having a bad cold or something and not going down there.

Then Marshall told how the state police provided with him a trooper as body guard. As Marshall left the courthouse with the trooper after meeting with Aldred, he found himself face to face with the police chief ...

And when he saw me he said, "Hi, you black son of a bitch, I've got you." And I ran. The state trooper pulled out his gun and said to the chief, "You stay right there."

Marshall left Dallas safely.

In Freeport, Long Island, Marshall asked a reporter to go with him as he investigated charges of harassment by police. Members of the Klan, who were often policeman as well, followed their car as they drove around collecting affidavits. The reporter was terrified. He told friends later: "... we had to keep dodging them all night ... even passed 'em a few times going in the opposite direction."

As they drove along, Marshall made outlandish jokes about what the Klan would do if they caught them.

Even though he joked about such incidents, Marshall had a bag of tricks to help him avoid dangerous situations. One trick was to swap automobiles frequently to confuse anyone attempting to follow him. Other tricks were to stay in a different house every night, or to eat supper at one house and slip away to another to sleep. Those who sympathized with the cause learned to respond to the call "Men are needed to sit up all night with a sick friend." This meant that Marshall needed an all-night bodyguard.

Chapter Four
"I remembered every lynching story."

In 1939, Marshall was appointed director-counsel for the NAACP's newly organized Legal Defense and Educational Fund, Inc. The name of the office was too long; it quickly became known as the Fund. Marshall explained the new department: "We get either a letter or a telephone call or telegram from either a person or a lawyer saying that they have a problem involving discrimination ... and it appears to be a legal problem."

This was a perfect job for Marshall. His ability to relate to blacks and whites at every level of society was a key to solving problems.

A lawyer who worked with him remarked on his "deep and real affection for the people he called the Little Joes," she said. "At a national convention, some little fellow might ask a not very penetrating question and ... someone else might wave him off. But Marshall would go see him himself because he knew that question was terribly important to this Little Joe, even if not to anyone else."

In 1941, he defended an African American, W. D. Lyons, who was jailed for setting a fire which killed white Elmer Rogers, his wife, and two children. After a year in jail, Lyons confessed to arson. Lyons' supporters suspected that police had forced the confession.

They called the Fund for help. NAACP members asked Marshall to take the case. They agreed to provide body guards and a different lodging each night.

Although many were afraid to host Thurgood, one elderly widow was not. "I ain't scared," she said as she welcomed him. She may not have been frightened, but Marshall was. Later he wrote, "during that first night I lay on the bed sweating in fear. I think I remembered every lynching story that I read ...."

At the trial, Marshall presented evidence that Lyons confessed only because police beat and terrorized him. Marshall showed the jury a photo of a police officer smiling as he stood over Lyons who lay on the floor, crumpled and bloody. Marshall questioned police officers who admitted throwing charred bones from the bodies onto Lyon's lap in order to make him confess. One of Marshall's witnesses reported hearing police talking about using a special type of blackjack called a "nigger beater" on Lyons.

In spite of this evidence, an all-white jury found Lyons guilty of murder. He was sentenced to life imprisonment.

NAACP lawyers appealed the sentence to the Supreme Court. The lawyers said that the jury had listened only to Lyon's confession. Jurists had paid no attention to the fact that the confession was forced.

The Supreme Court, all white men, agreed with the jury. They upheld the conviction.

Marshall was devastated. He declared that "The whole damn court system was stacked against Afro-Americans, other minorities, poor whites—all but the rich who were members of the same clubs as the judges, the fancy lawyers, the newspaper editors."

For many years after that, Marshall sent Lyons a few dollars at

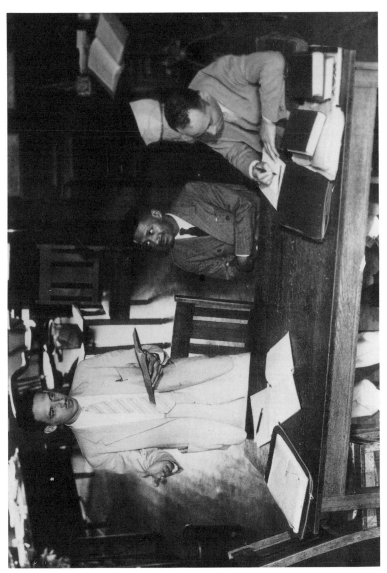

Young lawyer Thurgood Marshall argues a case. (Library of Congress)

Christmas, saying, "... use this to buy some candy, or cigarettes, or whatever you need most."

Marshall argued against the death penalty, no matter what the crime. He insisted that executions were undertaken "for no real reason other than to satisfy some vague notion of society's cry for vengeance." Besides, the sentence was most often imposed on "the poor, the ignorant, and the underprivileged members of society."

In a more light-hearted way, he explained his position like this:

> It's the old story about the man who was arguing with the hunter, and he said, "It's a shame, the way you shoot those poor little rabbits." He said, "Well, what do you complain' about? You go fishing every weekend." And the guy said, "Yeah, but the fish, it doesn't hurt the fish." And he said, "Have you ever asked a fish?"

Marshall then made his point: "Well, it's the same way about these people that are electrocuted and gassed and all. Some say it doesn't hurt them. Has anybody asked them?"

National events affected Marshall's work when the United States entered the Second World War in 1941. African Americans were accepted in every branch of the service. However, all units were segregated, as were post exchanges, bus service, and recreational facilities. Black soldiers reported hundreds of cases of discrimination. They said they were sentenced to harsh punishments for minor offenses while whites were either acquitted or given light punishments for the same offenses.

Marshall was not drafted into military service. He said, "I think the people on my draft board agreed secretly that they didn't need a damned troublemaking lawyer in the military ....But every day I knew that I was in the army, in heart and spirit, when I got an endless string of telephone calls, telegrams, letters, from colored GIs, or their wives, partners, girlfriends.... heart-wrenching stories of bigotry .... Nobody was into that war more than I was."

Wherever he traveled, Marshall was protected by NAACP bodyguards. They took security measures whenever they suspected trouble. Marshall was always assured of safe housing.

Once when he was investigating a lynching in Mississippi, he feared that he might be lynched himself, despite the bodyguards. He disguised himself as a farm worker.

Another time in Mississippi, he wanted to get a snack before his train left:

... this white man came up beside me in plain clothes with a great big pistol on his hip. And he said, "Nigger boy, what are you doing here?" And I said, "Well, I'm waiting for the train to Shreveport." And he said, "There's only one more train comes through here, and that's the 4 o'clock, and you'd better be on it because the sun is never going down on a live nigger in this town." I wasn't hungry anymore.

- Marshall had learned well the lesson that there were times when he had to accept being called a nigger.

Buster worried about her husband. Marshall was well aware of this. When anyone asked him how his wife felt about the threats he encountered, he said, "I think she took it the same way I did. If it happens, it happens."

When African Americans praised him for entering potentially

dangerous situations, he said, "I go into these places and I come out on the fastest vehicle moving. The brave blacks are the ones who have to live there after I leave."

Marshall believed that each court victory gave a feeling of power to those involved. But he was impatient, worried about the millions who were still treated as second-class citizens. "No matter how much education black people got," said Marshall, "they would remain semi-slaves until they got meaningful political power."

In the 1940s, fewer than 3% of eligible blacks in the southern U.S. voted. In many places, those who tried to register were ignored, threatened, humiliated, and rejected. In Alabama, for example, blacks who appeared at the registration desk were told they had to "understand and explain any article of the Constitution of the United States to the satisfaction of the registrars." Whites who appeared at the same desk were asked only to spell their names.

Marshall won a significant case in the right-to-vote struggle in 1944. The case involved Texas Democratic party rules that excluded non-whites from voting in primary elections. During this era, the Democratic candidate always defeated the Republican in the general election. The primary was the only chance for voters to send a message. In the case of *Smith v Allwright*, Marshall convinced the U.S. Supreme Court that all citizens had a right to vote in a primary election.

Marshall challenged the participants at an NAACP convention in 1944:

> The responsibility for enforcement of these [civil rights]
> statutes rests with every American citizen regardless of

A crowd watches as two men are lynched in Indiana in 1930. (Library of Congress)

race or color. However, the real job has to be done by the
Negro population ....

Although he had little money, Marshall was always careful about
his appearance. He paid attention to the way he looked so that nothing
would interfere with people's reactions to what he said and did. One
of his colleagues described him: "He wore natty, double-breasted
suits with immaculate white handkerchiefs sticking out of the breast
pocket; he had a neatly trimmed mustache ..."

Marshall laughed about a comment made on his hair style. He was
fighting pay discrimination for African American teachers in Louisiana and heard that a political boss had put out a $10,000 contract
on the life of "that burr-headed nigger lawyer from New York." When
he arrived in Louisiana to take the case, reporters asked Marshall what
he thought about the contract.

"Hell, I'm not burr-headed," he answered.

Reporters laughed, and that was the last anyone heard of the threat.

Marshall did not let personal humiliation interfere with his
NAACP work. "I ride in the for-colored-only cabs and in the back
of the street-cars—quiet as a mouse. I eat in Negro cafes and don't
use white washrooms. I don't challenge the customs personally
because I figure I'm down South representing a client—the NAACP—
and not myself."

When America and the Allies won the war in August, 1945,
Marshall hoped for a revolutionary change in American attitudes
toward racial equality. African American soldiers had shown brav-
ery, patriotism, and responsibility equal to white soldiers. "I couldn't
believe white Americans would continue to treat them [African

Americans] as semi-slaves.... I'd have bet a bundle that after the war [World War II] ... this country would move to place the colored race, in respect to civil rights, upon a level equal to whites." He would have lost that bundle. Discrimination flourished.

In the years directly after the war, Marshall traveled over fifty thousand miles annually. He joked about how much time he spent on trains. One Christmas his friends gave him a striped engineer's cap and an electric train set. He invited all the neighborhood kids to play with the train.

In 1945, NAACP leaders made a fateful decision. They decided to change their strategy. For years, they had fought to enforce the *Plessy v Ferguson* ruling, insisting that facilities for African Americans should be equal to those for whites. The new strategy focused on the belief that separate facilities could never be equal since no two situations could ever be the same. Marshall said, "The only way to get equality is for two people to get the same thing, at the same place and at the same time."

In 1946, Thurgood worked on a controversial case in Tennessee. Twenty-five African Americans were charged with assault and attempt to commit murder. A reporter asked him if he had police protection. Marshall answered: "They [the police] destroyed the Negro community. They slapped the Negroes around. They killed the two Negroes who were in jail. And I most certainly don't want them to protect me."

After appearing in court in Columbia, Tennessee, Marshall and a colleague named Looby were stopped at a roadblock. White policemen searched their car in vain for alcohol.

A few miles later, police stopped them again. Marshall told the story:

> Then I heard a voice in the back say, 'That's the one! The tall yalla nigger!' So they took me out toward the river and told Looby and the other guys to keep going the other way. Looby wouldn't go the other way. He was one brave man. He followed them as they carried me down toward the river. When we got down to the river bank, you could see the people [ready] for the party. By party, I mean lynch party. But Looby and the others wouldn't leave, so the whites didn't know what to do.

Next, the police accused Marshall of being drunk. They took him and Looby back to Columbia in a police car. The driver stopped the car in front of a building with a sign that said Justice of the Peace. He ordered Marshall to go into the building.

Marshall refused. "I'm not going to go over there so you can shoot me in the back and claim that I was escaping. That's too easy. You come with me."

An officer accompanied Marshall into the building:

> The magistrate turned to me and said, "Look, I'm a teetotaler. I've never had a drink in my life. If you're willing to take my test, I'll decide your guilt or innocence." "What's your test?" I asked. "Blow your breath in my face," he said. So I blew my breath, and the magistrate rocked a little bit and looked at the cop and said, "You're crazy. This man hasn't even had a drink."

Marshall always ended this story with: "After that, I really needed a drink."

The trial continued, and Marshall won acquittal for all twenty-five defendants.

That same year, doctors hospitalized Marshall for exhaustion. They warned he could have a relapse if he continued to work so hard. Sometimes he tried to pace himself a little more reasonably, but most of the time he simply could not afford to slow down. Besides, there was a more serious problem in the Marshall family. Buster did not feel well, either, and the doctors could not find the cause.

Chapter Five
"It ain't over yet, baby."

Marshall appeared before the U.S. Supreme Court in 1948 to defend Ada Sipuel, who was not admitted to the University of Oklahoma Law School because of her race. The case was *Sipuel v Oklahoma State Board of Regents*. Marshall argued that Sipuel was not receiving consideration equal to that of white applicants.

The Regents acted quickly to open a law school for African Americans. They set aside a room in the capitol, named it the Langston University School of Law, and hired four lawyers as part-time faculty. Langston University was obviously not equal to the University of Oklahoma Law School. Ada Sipuel refused to apply.

Marshall took the case back to the Court. He argued that Oklahoma's decision did not respect the *Plessy v Ferguson* ruling that demanded equal education for all races. The justices refused to consider Marshall's appeal. They said that Sipuel had sued for admission to law school. She had not specifically demanded a school equal to that of the whites. Since she was admitted to a law school, that case was closed.

The same year that Marshall argued the Sipuel case in the Supreme Court, he argued the McLaurin case in the federal district court that served Oklahoma. George McLaurin sued the Oklahoma State Board of Education for rejecting his application to the graduate school of education.

After the Board was found guilty of discrimination, they admitted McLaurin to the University of Oklahoma. However, they made many restrictions. For one class, his seat was in a broom closet. In the library, he could read only in a special section. At the campus snack bar, he could eat only at noon, when white students were barred from entering. He was allowed to use only specially designated toilet facilities.

Marshall did not accept either the Sipuel or McLaurin decisions as all-out defeats. At this point, he couldn't force state boards to provide equal schools, but he could force them to spend lots of time and money pretending to do so.

The next year, seventy-five African Americans registered for graduate classes in Oklahoma State University. The quickly constructed Langston University was insufficient in faculty and space. Officials had no choice but to accept the students at Oklahoma State University.

Accepting these new registrants was expensive. Most white students would not consider eating in the same cafeterias, living in the same dorms, swimming in the same pools, or using the same gym facilities. College officials quickly installed separate and unequal facilities.

Some citizens of both races asked why the NAACP spent so much time and money on graduate school problems. Wouldn't younger students gain more from integration than older ones? Marshall answered:

> Those racial supremacy boys somehow think that little kids
> of six or seven are going to get funny ideas about sex and
> marriage just from going to school together. But for some
> equally funny reason, youngsters in law school aren't
> supposed to feel that way. We didn't get it but we decided
> if that was what the South believed, then the best thing for
> the movement was to go along.

Marshall sued the state of Texas on behalf of Heman Sweatt, an African American who was rejected by the University of Texas Law School. Knowing they had to respond to the Plessy decision before the U.S. Supreme Court, Texas officials offered Sweatt admission to a "law school" they created with two rooms and a part-time instructor.

The U.S. Supreme Court handed down the *Sweatt v Painter* decision on April 3, 1950. Heman Sweatt must be admitted to the University of Texas School since the Regents could not provide an equal education in another school.

One day later, the Court heard Marshall's appeal of the McLaurin case. In that appeal, the justices ruled that University of Oklahoma officials had acted unconstitutionally. They could not force McLaurin to use facilities separate from whites. The forced separation prevented McLaurin from receiving the same benefits as white students.

Both the Sweatt and the McLaurin rulings were important steps on the road to overturning *Plessy v Ferguson*.

Marshall became known as a lawyer who would pursue a case until he achieved his goal. He had other fame as well. The *Afro-American* newspapers said that Marshall was the "amazing type of man who is liked by other men and probably adored by women." 'Some reporters called him "Mr. Civil Rights." The *Baltimore Afro-American* called him "The nation's biggest race man," noting that he was bigger than others in size as well as in status. He was six-foot-two, and had recently gained thirty pounds.

His story-telling reputation followed him. Friends and relatives learned to recognize the beginning of a story. He would draw a deep breath and begin, "You know ...."

One of his favorite stories was about an exclusive whites-only restaurant. Marshall said he told a (white) judge that he had been in the same whites-only restaurant as the judge. He had eaten the same wonderful meal and drunk the same expensive wine. There was only one difference, he told the judge. "You had yours in the dining room, and I had mine in the kitchen."

His sense of humor was just as bright as ever, but Marshall was over-working. He handled as many as six appeals to the U.S. Supreme Court at the same time, while also handling lower court cases. A fellow NAACP worker said, "The broadest shoulders of all belonged to Thurgood." Thurgood traveled about sixty thousand miles a year. Buster said, "He's nervous now where he used to be calm. This work is taking its toll of him. You know, it's a discouraging job he's set himself."

At forty-three, Marshall was over-weight. His long face sagged. Often his suits were wrinkled from hours and hours of traveling. *Newsweek* magazine called him "a rumpled bear of a man."

When someone praised Marshall for his successes, he said, "The only reason I look good is that I get expert advice and take it." However, he did confide to close friends that he worked with special care when talking to justices of the Supreme Court: "I ain't no fool when it comes to those boys."

Whenever he traveled to Washington, Marshall enjoyed getting together with old friends from Howard, NAACP officials and members, and lots of others. "Thurgood was a good poker player who had refined the art of the bluff," reported a friend. "... his heavy eyelids and the glare from his glasses made it difficult to tell if he was holding aces or if his hand was a total bust."

In May 1950, Harry Briggs, Sr. and his wife sued the Clarendon County, South Carolina schools on the grounds their children were not receiving educational services equal to those of white children. Marshall agreed to take the case. He found that the county spent nearly 100 times more for white students than for the black students. The hearing was scheduled for spring 1951 in the United States District Court for eastern South Carolina.

In January of that year, Marshall received urgent requests to study discrimination problems of African American soldiers in Korea. In that southeast Asian country, American military forces were helping South Koreans battle against a Communist take-over. So, while preparing for the Brigg's trial, Thurgood took a trip to Asia.

In Japan and Korea, Marshall spoke to hundreds of African American soldiers. They told him of harassment from officers, such as the officer who told them: "I despise nigger troops, and I don't want to command you, and the regiment is no good, and you are lousy." He investigated records of trials in which African American soldiers were sentenced to life imprisonment. Some of these trials were completed in less than an hour. He appealed cases for 40 men in the military courts, and achieved reduced sentences for 22 of them.

Marshall met with General Douglas MacArthur, commander of American troops in Korea. He asked the general why there were no African American officers on his staff or in any leadership positions. MacArthur answered that no blacks were qualified. Next, Marshall asked why there were no African Americans in the military band: "Don't you tell me there's no Negro that can play a horn!" MacArthur refused to answer. "That's when he said for me to go," Marshall said.

Back in the United States, Marshall and a group of activists boarded the train for Charleston, South Carolina to take part in the Briggs trial. At the Charleston station, a small group of parents, teachers, farmers, and others waited to welcome them.

Suddenly a short black man rushed through the heaps of luggage on the platform, shouting "Don't let the train leave. I forgot my dolls!" The man rushed to the railroad car and took out a large suitcase.

He was Dr. Kenneth Clark, a psychologist who used the dolls in an experiment with youngsters. His four dolls were identical except that two were brown and two were white. He asked three-to seven-year-old children which doll they liked best. Dr. Clark reported that both races preferred the white doll and rejected the brown one. He said that this showed that children of both races assumed white children must be superior. Dr. Clark concluded that segregated schools planted a stigma, a token of disgrace, in African American youngsters. That stigma remained with them throughout their lives, damaging their hopes for the future.

Marshall and Dr. Clark planned to use the doll experiments in the trial. They would show that the Briggs children suffered from a stigma, both in their own minds and in the minds of whites with whom they came in contact.

Marshall explained: "I told the staff that we had to try this case just like any other one in which you would try to prove damages to your client. If your car ran over my client, you'd have to pay up, and my function as an attorney would be to put experts on the stand to testify to how much damage was done. We needed exactly that kind of evidence in the school cases."

The group settled into "headquarters," a basement game-room in the private residence of NAACP supporters. Crowds of lawyers, reporters, witnesses, and local well-wishers appeared in the basement at all hours. A psychologist described the briefing sessions:

> [Marshall] would pose a question—often enough in a deliberate Negro dialect—that he anticipated the state might ask in the next day's court session. One of his staff members would suggest a possible reply and perhaps cite a precedent or two. Marshall would then lay into that staff member, spell out counter-arguments, refer to counter-citations, and completely destroy, or so I thought, the staff member's answer. The staff would then offer a rebuttal, Marshall would rebut the rebuttal, and this went on and on—between beer and sandwiches and coffee—to Marshall's seemingly huge amusement.

Soon after sunrise on May 28, 1951, African Americans from all over eastern South Carolina streamed into Charleston. They crowded into the federal building where the trial would begin at ten o'clock. Soon the courtroom was packed; those who could not find seats sat on benches in the hallway.

During the trial, plaintiffs cited conditions in the schools in the county. They told of a 600-pupil Negro school with only two toilets—both outdoors—and of a school where the only drinking water came from a nearby home. The defendants eventually admitted the schools were unequal and promised to improve conditions in black schools.

The judges ruled against the blacks, citing a "racial conflict heritage" which could not be erased easily. They did require that the officials of the Clarendon County school board furnish equal educational facilities. Those officials were ordered to report to the court on their progress in six months. But Marshall was not fooled. He knew the school board would do little to improve the schools. He felt pain, anger, and frustration although he admitted that he never expected to win. After reading a Charleston newspaper editorial praising the court decision his anger temporarily overcame him: "I slammed that *News and Courier* editorial on the floor and stomped on it, and I talked to it and said, 'It ain't over yet, baby!'"

Despite these fighting words, he confided to Dr. Clark: "You know, Kenneth, sometimes I get awfully tired of trying to save the white man's soul."

Tired or not, Marshall immediately filed an appeal of *Briggs v Elliott* with the U.S. Supreme Court.

Chapter Six
"We hit the jackpot!"

Three days later, the case of *Brown v Board of Education of Topeka* was heard in the United States District Court for Kansas. Oliver Brown was suing the Topeka, Kansas Board of Education because his daughter Linda had to walk six blocks, and then take a bus to the segregated school two miles away. He demanded that Linda be allowed to attend the school nearest her home, which was only four blocks away. Marshall kept up with the news on this case although he did not have time to work on it.

The court ruled that the Topeka Board of Education could require Linda to go to a segregated school. They contended that African American schools in Topeka were equal in quality to white schools. Linda had a right to an education, but members of the Topeka School Board had the right to choose where she would get that education.

On behalf of Oliver Brown, Marshall appealed to the U.S. Supreme Court. In January 1952, the Court refused to hear his appeal.

Despite his heavy work schedule, Marshall kept a personal interest in his clients. Once he defended a young black man sentenced to death for beating a white man and for kidnapping and raping his wife. Marshall was sure his client was innocent, but an all-white jury found him guilty. With tears in his eyes, he told the defendant's mother, "Don't worry, darling, we're going to stick by you. We are going to keep on fighting." Marshall was able to persuade the governor of Florida to change the death sentence to one of life imprisonment.

In the spring of 1952, South Carolina officials reported to the court on the Briggs case. They said that Clarendon County had "proceeded promptly and in good faith" to create better schools for African American youngsters. The court agreed. As the court session ended, an attorney for South Carolina told Marshall, "If you show your black ass in Clarendon county again, you'll be dead."

Marshall did not let threats stop him. He was determined to force the U.S. Supreme Court to over-turn the *Plessy v Ferguson* decision. He combined five cases against school segregation in one suit named Brown (after Oliver and Linda Brown) and four other plaintiffs who attended segregated schools. He was determined to prove that separate education, even where it seemed to be equal, violated the 14th Amendment. The U.S. Supreme Court scheduled a hearing for December 9, 1952.

That September, after months of working on briefs, Marshall called together 75 experts in fields as varied as history, economics, and psychology to add their resources to his arguments. Together, they discussed the invisible effects of segregated schools—including the damage to personality development, intellectual curiosity, and self-confidence.

By late November, Marshall was ready to try out his arguments. He asked Howard professors, law students, and NAACP personnel to take part in mock trials. Pretending that he was in front of the Supreme Court, Marshall stated his case, explaining how segregated

The inscription on the Supreme Court building reads "Equal Justice Under Law". (Franz Jantzen, Collection of the Supreme Court of the United States)

schools damaged youngsters. The "audience" reacted with every argument they could think of to contradict Marshall's reasoning. After many long sessions, Marshall felt confident that he would do well arguing his case before the Court.

Before dawn on Tuesday, December 9, a line of would-be spectators, about half of them African American, stood on the steps of the U.S. Supreme Court, an impressive white marble building in Washington, D.C. with the inscription "Equal Justice Under Law" carved on front. Despite the chilly air the line stretched down the sidewalk.

Finally the big bronze doors were opened. They filed into the courtroom, a high-ceilinged room framed by twenty-four marble pillars. The color red dominated—deep red carpeting and drapes. The spectators quickly filled the 160 seats available to the public. About four hundred people remained outside in the corridor where they hoped to be able to see and hear.

Marshall was the third speaker. He stressed that he was not requesting the admission of a specific student to a specific school; he was asking for the end of racial segregation of schools.

He argued: "... the plain purpose and effect of segregated education is to perpetuate an inferior status for Negroes which is America's sorry heritage from slavery."

The opposing lawyer, John Davis, argued that segregation was a "great national policy" and that integration would harm white children.

Marshall answered:

> ... in the South, where I spend most of my time, you will see white and colored kids going down the road together to school. They separate and go to different schools, and they come out and they play together. I do not see why there would necessarily be any trouble if they went to school together.

Davis answered:

> We shall get a finer better balance of spirit; an infinitely more capable and rounded personality by putting children in schools where they are wanted...

Marshall did not accept this argument:

> Segregation of Negroes ... brands the Negro with the mark

of inferiority and asserts that he is not fit to associate with
white people.

Arguments continued for three days. The court adjourned on the
afternoon of Thursday, December 11, 1952.

Then the waiting began.

Six months later, in June 1953, the justices summoned all lawyers
involved in *Brown v Board of Education*. Instead of announcing the
long-awaited decision, they said that they needed more information.
One question they had was about the Constitution: did the writers of
the 14th Amendment mean that school segregation was unconstitutional? Another question was about the process of integration: if
segregated schools became unconstitutional, what methods would be
used to integrate schools?

The lawyers were asked to return with the answers to those
questions in October, 1953.

"My heart dropped to my feet," Marshall remembered. Then he
realized that they had not lost the case. They had won another chance
to state their argument.

Marshall began work on the 14th Amendment question immediately. He was determined to prove that "there can be no doubt that
the framers [of the Fourteenth Amendment] were seeking to secure
and to protect the Negro as a full and equal citizen subject only to
the same legal disabilities and penalties as the white man."

Lawyers from all over the country sent research they hoped would
help. Luckily, Marshall was a quick reader. He could scan a report
and give an instant assessment like "Yeah, page five is great for us,
but page seven can kill us."

Office workers kept the mimeograph machine humming, making copies of notes, memos, and rough drafts. Everyone worked late. Sandwiches, coffee, and beer were the staples at every meal. One lawyer who participated wrote about Marshall: "I have *never* seen a man work so long and so hard. It was nothing for him to say at one a.m., 'How about a fifteen-minute break?'"

Marshall kept the humor flowing. At a pause in one meeting, most of the participants ordered chocolate milkshakes. A white professor ordered a vanilla one. Marshall roared, "We'll have no white chauvinism around here."

He told and re-told stories like the one where a Southern judge asked him, "What do you want from this court?" Marshall said he answered, "Anything I can get, your honor."

Sometimes he made remarks that embarrassed people. A white researcher borrowed Marshall's cigarette lighter but couldn't make it work. Marshall lit the cigarette for him, saying, "No way you can operate that—this here's a lighter I had made special for people who say niggers ain't mechanical."

Another time, he told a white researcher, "when we niggers take over the power, every time a white man takes a breath, he's gonna have to pay a fine." Nobody laughed. Later they talked about the comment among themselves. They agreed that Marshall was dramatizing to make the whites understand what it was like to daily face discrimination.

The *Brown v Board of Education* hearing was postponed until December, 1953 because of the sudden death of Chief Justice Fred Vinson. President Eisenhower replaced Vinson with the Governor of California, Earl Warren. The addition of Warren to the court would soon prove to be a major stroke of good luck for all those who, like Marshall, had worked so long to destroy legal segregation.

Marshall continued working on the case. Sometimes he felt satisfied; other times, he asked for help in presenting his case more forcefully or for more research. Finally, the 235-page brief satisfied Marshall. He filed it on December 5, 1953.

At one o'clock on the morning of December 7, a seventy-six-year-old son of former slaves was first in line on the steps of the Supreme Court. He remained alone in the thirty-degree weather until two o'clock, when a Howard law student joined him. By daybreak, long lines of people, both black and white, stretched along the sidewalk.

Just before the hearing opened, Buster and Marshall's mother were escorted to special seats in the hearing room.

John Davis, again arguing for the defense, opened by saying that the *Plessy v Ferguson* decision had been upheld over and over; there was no sense in re-arguing it now. To make his second point, he asked questions: "Would [integration] make the children any happier? Would they learn any more quickly? Would their lives be more serene?" He said the answer to all these questions was no. He went on to say that integration would create negative feelings that would harm children of both races.

The next day, Marshall answered Davis' last statement by repeating what he had said at the Briggs hearing: "Everybody knows that is not true." He answered other questions just as simply and directly.

Arguments continued for three days. The Court adjourned in the afternoon of December 9, 1953. Once again, lawyers on both sides would have to wait for a decision.

On May 17, 1954, Chief Justice Earl Warren called a news conference to announce the unanimous decision of the Court. First,

NAACP chief counsel Marshall holds a press conference, 1956. (Library of Congress)

he stated the question the Court had considered: "Does segregation of children in public schools solely on the basis of race ... deprive the children of the minority group of equal educational opportunities?"

He answered the question with just five words: "We believe that it does."

In the *Brown v Board of Education*, the justices ruled that segregated schools do create a feeling of inferiority.

When Marshall heard the decision, he leaned over to a fellow lawyer and whispered, "We hit the jackpot!"

Later he admitted that he had expected too much from the decision. "That was when we should have sat down and planned," he said. "The other side planned all the delaying tactics they could think of. And so they took the initiative .... we made a mistake, and I'm just as responsible for that as anybody else."

In some cities and towns in Maryland, Kentucky, and West Virginia, school boards began making plans for desegregation. A more typical reaction among Southern whites was expressed by the governor of North Carolina who said he was "terribly disappointed." The governor of Georgia said the Constitution was reduced to "a mere scrap of paper." A Mississippi senator declared that he would "not abide by or obey this legislative decision by a political court." Southerners opposed to integration adopted a rallying cry—"Never!" In Mississippi, Alabama, and Georgia, white "Citizens Councils" sprang up. Their goals and methods were much like those of the Ku Klux Klan.

The justices scheduled a hearing in April ,1955 to discuss implementation of their December ruling. Marshall knew this was his chance to insist on immediate desegregation of schools.

Before he could begin work on this project, he learned that Buster suffered from incurable cancer. For six weeks, he hardly left her side, fixing meals, changing bedpans, and refusing to see even his closest friends. His wife of twenty-five years died in February 1955. Marshall said, "I thought the world had come to an end."

His mourning was deep and agonizing. He needed more courage and determination than he had ever needed before. Yet even as he suffered, he knew that he must not allow grief to take over his life.

Two months after Buster's death, he was back in Supreme Court for hearings on how to enforce the decision against segregated education. The central question was: should school desegregation be gradual or immediate?

Marshall's team argued that integration should be immediate. Segregation was unconstitutional; there was no excuse for allowing it to continue.

Segregationists argued that integration should be gradual. Desegregation would create confusion, hostility, and perhaps, violence; there was no way the Court could force communities to open themselves to these problems.

Then segregationists brought up new controversy. They argued that African American children were educationally inferior to whites and that mixing the races would hurt white children.

Marshall refused to accept this excuse for not integrating. He countered: "Put the dumb colored children in with the dumb white children, and put the smart colored children with the smart white children—that is no problem."

Officials in Virginia added still another argument. They said that

African Americans were inferior in health as well as in academics. Marshall answered: "it is interesting to me that the very people ... that would object to sending their white children to school with Negroes are eating food that has been prepared, served and almost put in their mouths by the mothers of those children ..."

On April 16, the hearings ended, and the justices began deliberations. On May 31, 1955, they delivered their ruling: school systems were ordered to make a "prompt and reasonable start toward full compliance" and to proceed "with all deliberate speed."

Segregationists cheered. They knew that "prompt and reasonable" could be interpreted to mean whenever judges thought integration could work peacefully. A "start" could be the simple recognition that the Court had made a decision. "With all deliberate speed" could mean whenever legislators, school officials, and citizens were ready to consider working with the ruling. In other words, the ruling provided segregationists several ways to stall the original *Brown v Board of Education* decision outlawing segregated schools.

As Marshall left the Supreme Court building after the decision was announced, he squared his shoulders and said, "We're gonna be back. ... If we stop now, we're lost. They're going to try everything in the book to get out from under. Our job is to stay ahead of them. ... those white crackers are going to get tired of having Negro lawyers beating 'em every day in court." He declared that he and his team were willing to negotiate with officials about how and when desegregation would take place. However, he said, ".... we shall not negotiate as to *whether* it will take place."

He was optimistic: "We can be sure that desegregation will take place throughout the United States—tomorrow in some places, the day after in others, and many, many moons hence in some, but it will come eventually to all."

Marshall's father had always had faith in the Constitution. Now his son echoed that faith: "Law can change things for the better, moreover it can change the hearts of men, for law has an educational function also." He set the tone for this change: "We shall resort to the courts and ballot ... we shall do this peacefully, lawfully, and in the true American tradition."

One day he met Cecilia "Cissy" Suyat, a secretary at the NAACP office. A few months later he proposed to her and in December, 1955 they were married.

At first glance, Cissy and Marshall were very different. He was nineteen years older and over two feet taller. But in heart and mind, they were much alike. They had a lot in common—ideals, friends, and love of books and music.

Marshall still enjoyed cooking. One of his favorite dishes was "Turkish Delight," a combination of tomatoes, bacon, peppers, olives, cheese, and macaroni. Cissy liked his cooking. "Heaven knows what goes in the pot, but it comes out delicious!" she said.

When asked about women's rights, Marshall referred to Cissy. "I have always been in favor of women's rights, of complete and absolute equality, and that is to bring my wife down to my level." Soon the Marshalls had two sons, Thurgood, Jr. and John.

Chapter Seven
"They really don't hate me."

In the last month of 1955 the fight for civil rights entered a new stage. On December 1, in Montgomery, Alabama, Mrs. Rosa Parks was arrested for refusing to give her seat to a white man. By the next night, the leaders of the city's black community met at the Dexter Avenue Baptist Church to plan a boycott against the bus system. The church's young pastor was named Martin Luther King, Jr.

Over the next weeks, months and eventually years, the demand for racial justice was carried to the streets of cities all over the South. A new, more volatile stage of the long struggle for legal equality had begun.

Marshall did not take active part in this phase of the struggle. He thought boycotts would lead to more violence and bitterness. He wanted to fight discrimination in ways which would get people out of jail, not get them in. He continued pursuing justice in the courts.

In 1957, Congress discussed a civil rights bill to protect the voting rights of African Americans. During the discussion, segregationist senators, such as Richard Russell from Georgia, changed the wording to weaken the bill.

Once again, Marshall was disappointed by the high officials of the

15-year old Elizabeth Echford is denied entry into Little Rock's Central High School, 1957. (AP/Wide World Photos)

U.S. government, but he was not defeated. Believing that persistence would pay off, he said: "We've got the law, religion and God on our side, and the devil is on the other side."

Anti-integration groups sprang up and flourished; membership in the Ku Klux Klan grew. The White Citizens Councils, led mostly by Southern business leaders, swore to make it "difficult, if not impossible, for any Negro who advocates desegregation to find and hold a job, get credit, or renew a mortgage." Mobs of whites blocked school entrances in Kentucky, Tennessee, West Virginia, and Arkansas.

In Little Rock, Arkansas, school officials admitted just nine African American students to a white high school. They declared that this was evidence they were integrating.

When African American teenager Elizabeth Eckford arrived at the Little Rock school, a mob yelled, "No nigger bitch is going to get in our school."

Rioters beat reporters and journalists who accompanied the African American students. The mayor of Little Rock appealed to President Eisenhower for help.

Eisenhower ordered one thousand Army paratroopers to protect the students from violence. The African American students attended the school for a year, continually harassed, demeaned, and insulted. At the end of the year, Arkansas officials claimed they had proven that they could not integrate without losing law and order. Marshall was quick to answer: "Even if it be claimed that tension will result which will disturb the educational process, this is preferable to the complete breakdown of education which will result from teaching that courts of law will bow to violence .... it's only a question of time until integration is completed. We'll solve the problem peacefully—and gradually."

Congress considered another voting rights proposal in 1960. As with the 1957 bill, anti-black legislators watered it down until it was ineffective. Marshall studied the new proposal: "It would take two or three years for a good lawyer to get someone registered under this bill," he declared.

A feeling of despair settled over many African Americans. They saw little hope for change in white attitudes or actions. They were afraid of retaliation, more afraid than they were before they had made some gains in courts. These blacks urged their leaders to "go slow." Marshall snapped back: "They don't mean go slow. They mean don't go."

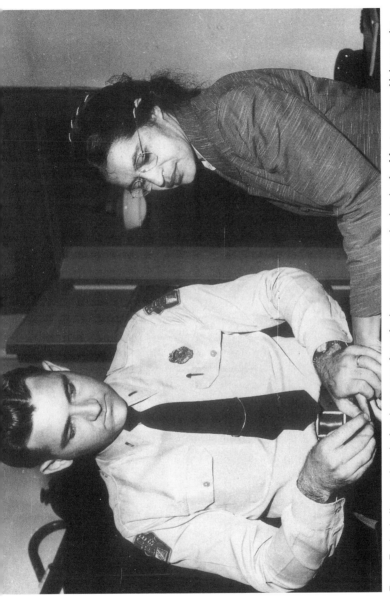

Rosa Parks is fingerprinted after her arrest for refusing to move to the back of a Montgomery, Alabama city bus. (AP/Wide World Photos)

Marshall traveled to Sierra Leone, Africa in 1961 as the personal representative of President John F. Kennedy. One hundred and twenty years earlier, Marshall's great grandfather had been dragged in chains from that country. Now Marshall was the official United States representative there.

That same year, Marshall helped officials of Kenya draft a constitution for their newly independent country. Part of his responsibility was to insure that the white minority was protected from the black majority. Marshall was on the other side of the fence for a change. "I'd give 'em the same protection a black man would want in Mississippi," he said.

He loved to tell this story about Kenya:

Police wouldn't let me speak to people. I said, "I wonder if I could just say a word to all those people out there." They said, "Nope, no speeches." I said, "I'm not going to make a speech. Just let me say one word of greeting." He said, "All right, all right, just one word." I said, "Okay," and I jumped up on top of this station wagon ... shouted out real loud one word, "Ururhu," and pandemonium broke out ... The reason was, the word ururhu means "freedom now." And he said, "I told you not to—" I said, "But I didn't say but one word."

In September 1961, President Kennedy asked Marshall to accept appointment as a judge on the United States Court of Appeals that served New York, Vermont, and Connecticut. Judges on the circuit courts are responsible for deciding which appeals should be sent up to the United States Supreme Court.

Marshall with Kenya premier Jomo Kenyatta in 1963. (Library of Congress)

Marshall hesitated to leave the NAACP just as it was gaining strength and winning cases against segregation in housing, public accommodations, and schools. Still, he said "when one has the opportunity to serve his government, he should think twice before passing it up."

He accepted the nomination, knowing that Congress might not approve his appointment. Southern legislators had not forgiven him for bringing integration into their cities and towns.

The Congressional hearing on Marshall's nomination began in January, 1962. Conflict was apparent right from the beginning. Senator James Eastland of Mississippi, one of the Senate's leading segregationists, persuaded other senators to shelve the appointment for further study. Finally, Eastland worked out a deal. He would vote for Marshall if Kennedy would appoint Eastland's friend Harold Cox to a federal judgeship. Eastland explained to Robert Kennedy, the President's brother, who was the U.S. Attorney General: "Tell your brother that if he will give me Harold Cox, I will give him the nigger." The deal was made.

Late in August 1962, almost a year after Kennedy nominated him, Marshall was confirmed by nearly three-fourths of the votes in the Senate.

When he was asked about the Southerners who worked against his appointment, he said: "They really don't hate me as a person ... I'm just a symbol to them—a symbol of something that is destroying their view of the Constitution. Lord help them! Some day they'll see the light."

As he left the NAACP offices, a reporter asked him if he ever got frustrated. "I guess the answer is, I should have been frustrated," he replied. "But you couldn't because all you could do was to push with what you had. If you give up, you're gone."

As federal judge, Marshall worked on cases involving civil, criminal, and tax laws. He was as busy as ever, but he was free from threats of local judges and other officials, and he no longer had difficult travel schedules. "I enjoy the slower pace behind a fancy desk, but I miss the excitement," he said.

In four years on the federal bench, Marshall wrote more than a hundred opinions. Many of his decisions involved the rights of individuals: teachers who objected to mandatory loyalty oaths; aliens who fought deportation; citizens who complained of illegal search and seizure. Some of his opinions became law.

His job as judge gave him more time to be with Cissy and their

Federal judge Marshall poses with his wife Cissy and sons. (Library of Congress)

two sons, Thurgood, Jr. and William. The boys and their father played with trains, went to cowboy movies, and simply sat and talked. Every Sunday the family attended services at the Episcopal Church together.

Throughout the country, racial violence increased. White terrorist groups planted bombs, set fires, and committed murders. African Americans and supportive whites formed groups to fight against the terrorism. In August 1963, a quarter of a million people, including 60,000 whites, marched in Washington in support of civil rights laws.

This was the beginning of the turbulent 1960s. In November, 1963 President John Kennedy was assassinated in Dallas. Halfway around the world, American soldiers were dying in alarming numbers in Vietnam. And throughout the South, Martin Luther King, Jr. and other non-violent protesters were beginning to tumble down the walls of segregation and oppression. An era of dramatic social change was taking place, and much of it was due to the years of work Marshall and his allies had done during the preceding decades.

One day in July 1965, Marshall was enjoying lunch with friends. A law clerk interrupted to tell him that the president had called.

The president of what? asked Marshall.

The president of the United States, answered the clerk.

Marshall leisurely finished his lunch and then returned the White House call. President Lyndon Johnson asked Marshall to become solicitor general of the United States.

The solicitor-general has two basic responsibilities. One is to defend the government when a person or organization sues the country in the U.S. Supreme Court. The other responsibility is to confer with the Supreme Court about which cases it should hear and how it should conduct the proceedings.

Marshall considered President Johnson's offer carefully. Obviously the appointment was an honor, a recognition of Marshall's competence and effectiveness. It was also a recognition by the country's highest official that an African American deserved respect.

However, there were disadvantages to the new job. Marshall would have to give up a life-time appointment as judge. He would have to take a $5000 cut in salary.

"I told Cissy that ... it might mean she couldn't get a new dress for a year, and all she said was 'So?' I told the boys they would have to cut back, too, but all they asked was if they would get to see me in court in the cutaway suit worn by solicitors general."

Marshall made up his mind. He explained: "I accepted because the President of the United States asked. ... Negroes have made great advancements in government, and I think it is time they started making some sacrifices."

President Johnson offered, and Marshall accepted the job, but those acts did not make him solicitor general. First, he had to be confirmed by the Senate. Some Democratic and Republican leaders wanted immediate confirmation. They saw no need for heavy questioning because they knew Marshall from his work with the NAACP and the U.S. Court of Appeals.

Other senators asked about Marshall's personal life, bringing up stories of heavy drinking, all-night poker games, fondness for baseball and western movies, and chain smoking.

Marshall answered easily: "Once in a while I'll catch a western on television, and I am still waiting to see one where the Indians win .... And poker, ha, I haven't pushed a chip in ten years. You know what cards I'm down to now? I play War with my two boys. Now that's hot action for you, isn't it?"

His nomination was approved by a vote of 69-11.

On August 24, 1965, Thurgood Marshall was sworn in as the first African American Solicitor General of the United States. President Johnson announced: "Our nation has now progressed to the point—in large measure because of what Thurgood Marshall has done—that race no longer serves as a bar to the exercise of experience and skill."

The boys did not get to see their father in a cutaway after all. When Marshall was sworn in as solicitor general in August 1965, he wore a dark blue three-button suit.

As he settled into his new office in the Justice Department, Marshall added a few special touches—a ceremonial leopard-skin cape from Kenya, a radio (it was World Series time), and a bust of Frederick Douglass, who had fought for racial equality during the years before the Civil War.

For the first time in his life, Marshall had the support of some of the best lawyers in the country and all the money he needed to pursue cases. In October, Marshall was back before the Supreme Court. He yielded to tradition, wearing striped pants, a pearl-gray vest, and a cutaway coat. "Now isn't this the silliest getup in the world?" he asked.

No one would think to call Marshall silly. He was an impressive figure, over 6 feet tall and over 200 pounds with a neatly trimmed mustache and hair graying at the temples. His voice was deep, strong, and confident. His formal title was now Mr. Justice Marshall.

Friends asked him if he was nervous in his new position. As usual he answered in his mock voice:

Hell, I ain't had the jitters in the Supreme Court since de

Solicitor General Marshall and his family, President Johnson, and friends enjoy a joke. (Yoichi R. Okamoto, LBJ Library Collection)

day I was admitted to practice nearly thirty years ago. But
dat day, oh boy! You coulda heard mah knees knockin' way
out in de hall!

In November, he argued a case that was typical of many he
handled. Fifteen Ku Klux Klan members had been charged with
conspiring in the murders of three civil rights workers in Mississippi.
The state court dismissed the charges. Marshall argued that the men
should have been tried. He won his case and the charges were re-
instated.

In a similar case, Marshall argued for the government against the
state of Georgia. The state had dropped charges against whites
accused of the murder of African Americans during a Ku Klux Klan
raid. Solicitor General Marshall argued that the trial should be held,
and the Supreme Court agreed with him.

In another case, he argued against South Carolina, where state
officials declared that they, not the federal government, would
determine who could vote. The Supreme Court agreed with Marshall
that the 15th Amendment, which prohibited state and federal gov-
ernments from depriving any citizen of the right to vote on racial
grounds, rendered the South Carolina law unconstitutional.

Marshall argued against the state of California when it passed
legislation to allow discrimination in housing. Marshall successfully
argued that the United States Constitution over-ruled any state laws
that allowed discrimination.

Between 1965 and 1967, Marshall won fourteen of the nineteen
cases that he tried. When a reporter asked what he thought of this
record, he answered: "I volunteered to argue the toughest cases. I
guess my record is about as good as anybody else's."

Chapter Eight
"Oh, yipes!"

Many of the cases Marshall was involved with as Solicitor General concerned the Civil Rights Act of 1964. This act, which finally accomplished most of the goals of the earlier, weaker laws on civil rights, prohibited job discrimination on the basis of race, sex, or religion. It also prohibited racial discrimination in pubic accommodations like hotels, entertainment centers, and transportation terminals. The 1964 Civil Rights Act created anger and violence. Blacks complained about delays in its implementation. Resistant whites complained about changes in 200-year-old customs.

In the South, the threats, intimidation, beatings, lynchings, bombings, and murders escalated. Marshall urged African Americans not to retaliate in the same way. He insisted that the ballot was the most effective way to solve problems. He said, "Nothing will be settled with a rock ... It takes no courage to throw a rock. Rather, it takes courage to stand up on your own two feet and look anyone straight in the eye and say, 'I will not be beaten'."

Marshall sharply disagreed with former Vice President Richard Nixon, who said demonstrators showed a disrespect for law and should be punished. Marshall said, "I resented that crap....he [Nixon] wasn't trying to promote peace in the streets; he was playing politics with a volatile situation."

Marshall defended a citizen's right to privacy in a case involving wiretapping by the Federal Bureau of Investigation. As he worked on this case, he wondered if his own telephone had ever been tapped. He wondered, but he didn't worry. "All they [the FBI] would have heard was me cussing and my wife gossiping," he said.

On June 13, 1967, President Johnson called Marshall.

"I'm going to put you on the Supreme Court," he said.

"Oh, yipes!" answered Thurgood.

Johnson told him that the press conference announcing the nomination was at that moment being set-up in the Rose Garden. Would Thurgood accept a seat on the nation's highest court? Thurgood accepted.

In the Rose Garden announcement ceremony, Johnson said in a strong and determined voice: "I believe it is the right thing to do, the right time to do it, the right man, and the right place." Marshall, the great-grandson of a slave, heartily agreed.

Tradition came tumbling down with that nomination. Supreme Court justices had always been white, male, and Protestant with one exception (Louis Brandeis, a Jew). None of the justices had experienced segregation, been chased by the Ku Klux Klan, or defended blacks against charges of murder.

Southern Senators fought hard against Marshall's appointment. South Carolina Senator Strom Thurmond asked Marshall a string of sixty trivial, arcane questions about the Court. He hoped to convince people Thurgood, who had argued and won dozens of cases before the Supreme Court, was not intelligent or capable enough to serve. One example of Thurmond's strategy was the question: Do you know

Cissy helps her husband prepare for his 1967 Supreme Court swearing-in ceremony. (AP/Wide World Photos)

from what provision of the prior law the language of this [the 13th] Amendment was copied? Even some senators opposed to Marshall's nomination were shocked by Thurmond's tactics.

Despite the badgering from segregationist senators, Marshall was confirmed.

On October 2, 1967, the day of his formal appointment, the Marshall family watched from their reserved seats as President Johnson entered the Court room. The marshall of the Court pounded the gavel and announced "Oyez, oyez, oyez!" The eight justices entered from behind red velvet drapes and took their seats.

Fifty-nine-year-old Thurgood Marshall swore "to administer justice ... and to do equal right to the poor and to the rich ... according to the best of my abilities and understanding."

He accepted the formalities, interviews, and praise that were traditional for a new justice. But he was quick to down-play his importance. A few weeks after his swearing-in, he sat through a long recital of his accomplishments as he was introduced as a speaker. Then he opened his talk with a story:

> I'm thinking about a widow who was sitting in the church with her little boy, listening to the parson preach her husband's funeral services. The preacher said so many flowery things that she leaned down and whispered to her son, "go up there and look in the casket and see if that man the preacher is talking about is really your daddy!"

Once he played elevator operator in the Supreme Court building. Some white tourists accidentally got into an elevator reserved for the justices. When they saw Marshall in the elevator, they assumed he was the operator, and they told him what floor they wanted to get out on. Marshall bowed, said "Yassuh, yassuh," and pushed the button for their floor.

The question of free speech came up frequently in the Court. Several cases involved the right of a state to ban pornography. The justices were asked to define pornography, and to decide if a public display of such material was legal. Part of the research for this decision was watching allegedly pornographic movies. Marshall sat in a front seat and joked throughout the movies. "That was a fun assignment," he told a reporter. "Lots of fun. I really enjoyed it."

Marshall voted consistently for freedom of speech and against censorship. "If the First Amendment means anything, it means that a State has no business telling a man, sitting alone in his own house, what books he may read or what films he may watch."

Other cases concerned crime and crime prevention, gun control, threats of violent crimes, and forced confessions. Marshall had bitter memories of forced confessions and the W. D. Lyons case in 1941.

Americans were concerned about these questions and about other problems. Citizens debated and protested against United States involvement in the Vietnam War. This led to even more questioning about free speech, right to dissent, and loyalty and patriotism. Marshall worried about the increasing demonstrations. He repeated that usually these protests did more harm than good. He told students in New Orleans, Louisiana, "What I want to talk to you about this afternoon is ... not to stop this energy, but to channel it toward a decent end ....don't get mad—get smart!" He asked them to appreciate the fact that race relations had improved since the 1940s. However, he admitted, "I'm not going to be completely satisfied. I'll be dead before I'm satisfied."

He worried about the slogan: "Black is beautiful." "I don't believe that everything that's black is right and everything else is wrong. I think that we Negro Americans have just as many beautiful people in mind and body, as well as skin, as any other group. And I am sure we have just as many stinkers as there are in every other group."

In November 1968, the Marshalls decided to move from their mostly African American neighborhood to an all-white subdivision in Falls Church, Virginia. They bought a lovely 5-bedroom ranch-style house overlooking a lake. Since the Marshalls were the first non-white family on the block, reporters asked lots of questions. Marshall answered simply, "It's a private matter where I make my home."

In their new home, they often hosted large back-yard parties with plenty of chicken, spare ribs, and steaks. Marshall was especially pleased to live near the waterfront so he could buy bushels of blue-claw crabs to cook in his special broth of cider vinegar and seasonings. He played softball and football with his sons. Both Marshall and Cissy liked to go to the racetracks in Maryland. When the Baltimore Orioles were playing, he watched baseball games. During football season he and Cissy went to the Robert F. Kennedy Stadium to watch the Washington Redskins play.

Marshall disliked the changes in Court style that occurred after Warren Burger became Chief Justice in 1969. The new Chief, who was appointed by President Nixon, was much less concerned than Earl Warren had been about expanding constitutional rights to those traditionally left out of the mainstream of American society. In addition, he was stiffly formal, which was a marked contrast to Thurgood. Marshall believed that this attitude was inappropriate and

Justice Marshall poses before the Supreme Court. (AP/Wide World)

unnatural. When Marshall met Burger in the halls, he liked to tease him with a wave and a loud "What's shakin', chiefy baby?"

In 1969, fifteen years after the Brown decision, Americans still disagreed about how to achieve school integration. Marshall believed that the courts had to intervene. "When school boards fail to meet their obligations," he said, "it is up to the courts to find remedies that effectively secure the rights of Negro children."

President Nixon disagreed with most of Marshall's opinions. Nixon was eager to appoint a Court successor to Thurgood. In 1970 when Marshall was hospitalized for bronchitis, Nixon sent his aides to Marshall's doctor to ask for a report on the justice's health. Before the report left the hospital, Marshall scrawled on it in large red letters "NOT YET!"

Some war protestors were arrested for wearing clothes decorated with anti-war slogans and anti-American symbols. Marshall sided with the accused protestors, saying that freedom of speech includes freedom of dress.

As President Nixon and the man who succeeded him, Gerald Ford, appointed conservative justices to the Supreme Court, Marshall found himself more often in the minority. Unlike the other justices, Marshall had spent much of his life working with people who lived in poverty, unsure of the next job, meal, or housing opportunity. He understood the long-lasting effects of such insecurity and was not about to forget them now that he was a high government official. He had no difficulty understanding a plaintiff who argued he could not afford to pay a fifty dollar fee to file for bankruptcy. When five of the nine justices ruled that the plaintiff could pay the fee in weekly installments, Marshall was enraged. "It may be easy for some people to think that weekly savings of less than $2 are no burden," he wrote, "but no one who has had close contact with poor people can fail to understand how close to the margin of survival many of them are."

Marshall spoke freely about his philosophical differences with the other justices. "When young lawyers apply to clerk in my office," he said, "the first thing I ask is, 'Do you like writing dissents? If you don't, baby, this is not the office for *you*.'" He found it difficult to usually be on the losing side on most cases. But more importantly, he grew discouraged about what he saw as the country turning its back on the racial and economic inequalities that still existed.

Marshall was comfortable with his clerks, and they with him. He frequently invited them to his home for dinner on a Saturday night. They often shot pool together. His clerks, as well as the clerks of other justices, enjoyed his story-telling. One noted that Marshall was popular at informal parties. "Nearly half of the clerks were gathered around him [Marshall] listening to raucous tales while the rest of us discussed our law schools and geographic origins with other justices."

There was another side to this storytelling. Some of his clerks complained that Marshall over-did it. They said that he often visited them after lunch. He made himself comfortable in an easy chair in their office, and settled down to tell stories. One day a clerk decided to stop the stories before they began. He piled books on the comfortable chair "reserved" for Marshall. On that day, the justice, drawing on a life-time habit of standing for long hours in trials, stood to tell his stories.

Chapter Nine
"Prop me up and keep on voting."

In 1972 the Supreme Court was asked to decide: does the death penalty violate the Eighth Amendment's prohibition against "cruel and unusual punishments?"

Marshall answered Yes, and wrote a sixty-page document explaining his position. He used studies to prove innocent people were often sentenced to death. He also argued that the death penalty was enforced most often against minorities and poor people.

After heated argument, the Court arrived at a decision that pleased nobody. They decided that sentencing procedures needed investigation.

Marshall voted with the majority in the 1973 *Roe v Wade* case, which upheld a woman's right to have an abortion. Marshall said anti-abortion laws forced women to bear children who would suffer in misery and poverty.

He agreed with the Court decision to allow prison inmates to send mail without censorship. "When the prison gates slam behind an inmate, he does not lose his human quality .... a prisoner needs a medium for self-expression."

In August 1974, the Court heard a case from Detroit, Michigan.

The Detroit schools were still segregated, and school officials were ordered to follow a busing plan to integrate the schools. The officials asked that the order be cancelled. Marshall fought to retain the plan. He argued that "...unless our children begin to learn together, there is little hope that our people will ever learn to live together." But the Court voted to cancel the plan. An angry Marshall declared: "After 20 years of small, often difficult steps [toward equal justice under law] the Court today takes a giant step backwards."

Like the other justices, Marshall received death threats from citizens who objected to his rulings. A reporter asked Marshall how many threats he had received.

"Dunno," he replied, "but more than I've ever wanted to count."

In 1976, Marshall had a slight heart attack. He suffered bouts of both pneumonia and bronchitis. He was bothered by glaucoma, an eye disease which blurred his vision. The sixty-seven-year-old justice was overweight, smoked heavily, and occasionally drank too much.

Although forced to accept physical limitations, he continued to write opinions and to give speeches. One of his basic messages was that the Constitution could, and should, be an active force for the American people. "Over 200 years, it [the Constitution] has slowly, through our efforts, grown more durable, more expansive, and more just. But it cannot protect us if we lack the courage, and the self-restraint, to protect ourselves."

In one case, police department officials insisted that officers must have short hair. When a policeman took the case to court, the justices voted in favor of the police department. Marshall dissented. He wrote that an individual's personal appearance was a part of his personality.

In 1977, the city of Baltimore commissioned a sculptor to build an 8-foot tall bronze statue of Marshall to stand at the entrance to a new federal court house. When asked what he thought of the statue, Marshall was not ready to celebrate a victory of civil rights: "I just want to be sure that when you see this statue, you won't think that's the end of it. I won't have it that way. There's too much work to be done."

One of his most controversial opinions was in favor of affirmative action, the concept that persons who have been discriminated against deserve special consideration when applying for jobs or admission to colleges and graduate schools. Many schools and corporations had adopted this idea. In 1978, the Supreme Court heard the case of a white student, Alan Bakke, who sued against an affirmative action policy. He claimed that he was denied admission to a medical school because he was not a minority applicant. The majority on the Court ruled that the school's affirmative action program was unconstitutional because it discriminated against majority applicants.

Marshall disagreed with the Bakke decision. "The dream of America as the great melting pot has not been realized for the Negro; because of his skin color he never even made it into the pot... it [is] difficult for me to accept that Negroes cannot be afforded greater protection under the Fourteenth Amendment where it is necessary to remedy the effect of past discrimination."

Marshall was concerned with topics other than civil rights. His worked on technical opinions on federal income tax statutes, railroad legislation, and other matters.

Like their father, Marshall's sons were interested in law. Thurgood Marshall, Jr. graduated from the University of Virginia with a law degree. He worked for Senator Edward Kennedy and then became a legislative affairs coordinator in Vice-President Albert Gore's office. John, the younger son, earned a degree in government and sociology from Georgetown University in Washington, D.C. He became a state trooper specializing in firearms and survival tactics. Marshall spoke proudly of his children:

> I didn't give advice to either of my boys. I had a deal with them: I would answer any question, but I wouldn't give volunteer advice. And it ends up that one of them gave up a job paying $100,000 with the biggest law firm here to go to work for Ted Kennedy. I said, "With all the money I spent on your education, why did you take that?" You know what he said? "I know somebody else who didn't give a damn about money, too." My other son is a state trooper, a state policeman, and he had the same kind of education ... And you know what he said? "I want to work for the people."

At first, Marshall refused to attend a 1987 reenactment of the writing of the Constitution on the 200th anniversary of the signing. He said his only place at such a reenactment would be as a slave: "If you are going to do what you did 200 years ago, somebody is going to give me short pants and a tray so I can serve coffee." Then he changed his mind. After the reenactment scene, he gave a short speech, calling attention to the fact that the Constitution was "defective" because it had failed to abolish slavery and to give the right to vote to women.

He became increasingly disappointed with the slow pace of

integration in the United States. He said of some of his fellow justices, "They need to stop looking for excuses not to enforce the 14th Amendment ..... You can't name one member of this court who knew anything about Negroes before he came to this court .... What you have to do—white or black—you have to recognize that you have certain feelings about the other race, good or bad...."

He would not make optimistic speeches about the progress of civil rights for African Americans. He said, "The trouble is—if you haven't been a Negro, you don't understand. They think you're just 'sensitive' about something. Well, let's find out what you're sensitive about. When you're not eating, or you can't find a place to sleep, sure, you get sensitive."

Marshall was particularly concerned with police procedures. He could never forget being falsely accused of driving under the influence of alcohol. He was especially alert for proof of intimidation when plaintiffs complained of unwarranted searches, prejudiced questioning, and illegal evidence gathering. He was also sympathetic to citizens who did not have enough money to fight for their rights in courts.

But Marshall was fighting an up-hill battle. By the end of the 1980s, only one justice, William Brennan, voted consistently with Marshall. The only decision the whole Court agreed on, said Marshall, was breaking for lunch. Still, he wanted to stay on the Court as long as he could. He feared that his replacement might vote to change all that he had worked for. He told his clerks, "If I die, prop me up and keep on voting."

He continued to fight for a woman's right to have an abortion. In 1990, he wrote a dissenting opinion on a Court decision that a minor

Associate Justice Marshall shares a joke in his office. (Deborah Rhode, Collection of the Supreme Court of the United States)

had to notify her parents or a judge before having an abortion. Marshall said: "This scheme forces a young woman in an already dire situation to choose between two fundamentally unacceptable alternatives: notifying a possibly dictatorial or even abusive parent and justifying her profoundly personal decision in an intimidating judicial proceeding to a black-robed stranger."

By 1990, eighty-one-year-old Marshall's silver hair was thinning, his weight was constantly on the increase, and he wore two hearing aids. Occasionally tears, caused by glaucoma, would run down his face. Because of poor vision, he could no longer drive. Although he had to hold papers close to his eyes, he read constantly. He gave no interviews. He often failed to hear questions unless they were shouted, and he sometimes mumbled when spoken to. His family and friends worried about his history of heart problems and other physical infirmities, including a potentially dangerous blood clot in his leg.

Government leaders, law colleagues, and Marshall himself wondered how long he could perform his duties. Could he wait until the United States had a president who would fill his seat with someone who shared his views? The current president, George Bush, was an opponent of most of the civil right advances of the past two decades. Would Thurgood be forced to resign during the term of a president who would nominate someone with opposing opinions?

Reporters openly asked him about the possibility of his resigning. One interviewer asked if he thought that his replacement should be an African American. Marshall answered, "I think the next justice should be a qualified person."

At a dinner in his honor, Marshall pointed to a large photograph of himself. "...You know what worries me about this thing, and I ask you to look at it—doesn't it look like a memorial? Well, I've got news for you that I will try to put in the best English available: I ain't dead yet!"

He laughed at his jokes, but he could not ignore his health. He made an appointment at Bethesda Naval Hospital to have a pacemaker installed to stabilize his irregular heartbeat. "I'm still kickin', but not very high," he admitted.

On June 27, 1991, the eighty-two-year-old justice sent a note to President Bush:

My dear Mr. President,

The strenuous demands of court work and its related duties

required or expected of a justice appear at this time to be incompatible with my advancing age and medical condition. I, therefore, retire as an Associate Justice of the Supreme Court of the United States when my successor is qualified.

Respectfully,
Thurgood Marshall

At a press conference, he told reporters that he hoped that the President would not replace him with "the wrong Negro." It was evident he was upset about the possibility of being replaced with someone who would attempt to undo his life's work. He answered questions with sarcasm, impatience, and a touch of humor:

Reporter: How do you feel?

Marshall: With my hands.

Reporter: What's wrong with you, sir?

Marshall: I'm old. I'm getting old and coming apart.

Reporter: Do you have any plans for your retirement?

Marshall: Yep.

Reporter: What are they?

Marshall: Sit on my rear end.

Another reporter asked him about the status of black people. Marshall objected, "I am not a 'black people', I am an Afro-American. Now you want to talk about an Afro-American? No, I am not free, certainly I am not free. You know, everybody quotes Dr. Martin Luther King, Jr. as saying, 'Thank God, we're free at last. We're not free, we're nowhere near free. "

Marshall often told this story:

> Years ago a Pullman porter told me that he'd been in every
> state and every city in the country and he'd never been any
> place in this country where he had to put his hand up and
> feel his face to know that he was a Negro. I agree with him.
> Segregation is general, we still have it.

When he was asked what major tasks the Supreme Court faced
in the near future, Marshall answered, "To get along without me!"

A reporter asked what he would choose for his epitaph. Marshall
answered immediately, "He did the best he could with what he had."

Associate Justice Thurgood Marshall died from heart failure on
January 24, 1993.

Thurgood Marshall, Mr. Civil Rights, was once a youngster who
soiled himself because he was not allowed to use public restrooms
in Baltimore. He was also a teenager whose grandmother taught him
to learn to cook so he would always have an employable skill, an
honors graduate of Lincoln University who was refused admission
to the University of Maryland Law School because of his color, a
young lawyer who represented so many poor clients that he lost
money his first years of practice, an NAACP lawyer who was not
allowed to eat or sleep in Southern towns where he represented
clients, and, finally, a U.S. Supreme Court justice noted for his
concern for the poor, the powerless, and all those who were discriminated against.

Thurgood Marshall made a difference. He understood that just laws are the foundation of a just society. He was a model of courage and determination who insisted that the fight against discrimination be continued because, as he said, "If we stop now, we're lost."

Appendix
Selected Civil Rights Cases

Plessy v Ferguson (1896)

PLAINTIFF	DEFENDANT
Homer Plessy sued the state of Louisiana for refusing to allow him to sit where he wanted on a public train.	Judge John Ferguson said that Louisiana law allowed any citizen to travel on a train, but he could not choose his seat.

Arguments

The 14th Amendment says that no state can enforce a law which curtails the rights of a U.S. citizen.	The 14th Amendment does not guarantee social equality or mingling of the races.

Decision

Plessy lost. State laws may enforce separation of races as long as all citizens receive equal treatment.

Hocutt v University of North Carolina (1932)

PLAINTIFF	DEFENDANT
African-American Thomas Hocutt sued the University of North Carolina for rejecting his application for admission on racial grounds.	The University replied that state law did not require them to accept him.

Arguments

The 14th Amendment prevents states from enforcing laws curtailing the rights of U.S. citizens.	The university operated under state law and could not be controlled by the federal government.

Decision

Thomas Hocutt lost. He could not demand admission to the university.

Murray v The University of Maryland (1935)

PLAINTIFF	DEFENDANT
Donald Murray sued the Univeristy of Maryland Law School for rejecting him on racial grounds.	UM Law School officials said that state law prohibited them from admitting blacks.

Arguments

The *Plessy v Ferguson* decision required the state to furnish Murray with an education equal to that at UM Law School.	The law school admitted there was no black school in Maryland equal to the one at UM.

Decision

Murray won. The University of Maryland Law School was ordered to admit him.

7th Grade Student v Baltimore County Board of Education (1936)

PLAINTIFF	DEFENDANT
Marshall sued Baltimore County for refusing to allow a 7th grade student to attend the school nearest her home.	The state argued the student could attend the black-only school nearest to her home.

Arguments

The pupil should be allowed to attend any school she wanted.	The state was forced to offer her an education, not a choice of schools.

Decision

Marshall lost. The court ruled that the state could place students wherever they wished.

Smith v Allwright (1944)

PLAINTIFF	DEFENDANT
African-American Lonnie Smith sued because he was not allowed to vote in the Texas Democratic primary.	Texas election Judge S.C. Allwright decided that only members of the Democratic party could vote in the primary.

Arguments

The Democratic primary is part of the election process. All citizens are guaranteed the right to vote by the 15th and 20th Amendments.	The Democratic Party is a private organization and is therefore not regulated by state or national law.

Decision

Lonnie Smith won. The U.S. Supreme Court stated that voting is a constitutionally guaranteed right.

Sipuel v Oklahoma State Board of Regents (1948)

PLAINTIFF	DEFENDANT
Ada Sipuel sued the Oklahoma State Board of Regents for not admitting her to the state university law school.	The Regents said that state law prohibited admission of blacks to the Oklahoma State Univeristy Law School.

Arguments

The 14th Amendment forbids states from enforcing laws that curtail the rights of a U.S. citizen.	The Regents argued they had to obey state laws.

Decision

Ada Sipuel won. Oklahoma had to make a legal education available to Sipuel or to close its whites-only school.

McLaurin v Oklahoma State Regents for Higher Education (1948)

PLAINTIFF	DEFENDANT
George McLaurin sued the Oklahoma State Board of Education for refusing his admission to graduate school.	The Regents argued that state laws prohibited graduate schools from accepting black students.

Arguments

The 14th Amendment prevents states from enforcing laws curtailing the rights of U.S. citizens.	The university operated under state law and could not be controlled by the federal government.

Decision

George McLaurin won. The state was ordered to admit him to a graduate school of education.

Sweatt v Painter (1950)

PLAINTIFF	DEFENDANT
Heman Sweatt sued President Painter of the University of Texas because he was not admitted to a school equal to the University of Texas.	Texas officials would not break state law by admitting a black to the University of Texas.

Arguments

Separate facilities can not be equal because they do not offer the exact same opportunities to students.	Given time, the state would make the black school equal to the white school.

Decision

Heman Sweatt won. He could receive a "reasonable" legal education in Texas only at the University of Texas Law School.

Briggs v Elliott (1951)

PLAINTIFF	DEFENDANT
Henry Briggs sued Roderick Elliott because his daughter was forced to attend an all-black school where she was stigmatized.	Roderick Elliott, Chairman of the Clarendon County school board said they were in the process of equalizing black and white schools.

Arguments

Segregated education created stigmas which harmed black children.	South Carolina needed time to create an equal school system.

Decision

Briggs lost. *Plessy v Ferguson* upheld segregated schools, and the court believed that Clarendon County was working to make the schools equal.

Brown v Board of Education of Topeka (1954)

PLAINTIFF	DEFENDANT
Oliver Brown sued the Topeka, Kansas Board of Education for assigning his daughter to a segregated school.	The Topeka school board said that Linda Brown's education was equal to that received in white-only schools.

Arguments

Segregated education is necessarily inferior to integrated education.	The facilities, curricula, and teacher's pay are equal in white and black schools.

Decision

Oliver Brown won. The U.S. Supreme Court ruled that segregated schools do generate a feeling of inferiority in African American children.

TIMELINE

1908	—	born in Baltimore, Maryland.
1929	—	marries Vivian "Buster" Burey.
1933	—	graduates from Howard University with law degree and begins practicing in Baltimore.
1935	—	wins first major civil rights case (with Charles Houston).
1936	—	becomes assistant special counsel for NAACP.
1938	—	becomes counsel for NAACP.
1940	—	wins first case before the U.S. Supreme Court.
1951	—	travels to South Korea to investigate racism in the U.S. military.
1954	—	wins *Brown v. Board of Education of Topeka, Kansas* case, ending legal segregation in public schools.
1955	—	"Buster" dies; marries Cecilia Suyat.
1962	—	becomes a judge on the U.S. Court of Appeals.
1965	—	becomes U.S. Solicitor General.
1967	—	appointed to the U.S. Supreme Court.
1991	—	retires from U.S. Supreme Court.
1993	—	dies from heart failure.

GLOSSARY

acquit: to declare innocent.

affidavit: a written declaration made under oath.

affirmative action: belief that persons who have been discriminated against deserve special attention.

14th Amendment: includes the language "no state shall make or enforce any law which shall abridge the privileges of immunities of citizens of the United States"..."nor deny to any person within its jurisdiction the equal protection of the laws."

15th Amendment: includes the language "the right of citizens of the United States to vote shall not be denied or abridged ... on account of race, color, or previous condition of servitude."

appeal: request for a new hearing.

boycott: to refuse to do business with a company as a form of protest.

brief: document stating facts and points of law for a specific case.

capital punishment: death penalty imposed for a crime.

civil rights: rights granted to every citizen.

conviction: act of proving a person guilty in a court trial.

counsel: a lawyer or group of lawyers.

defendant: a person accused in court of wrongdoing.

desegregate: to end racial separation.

discriminate: to make judgements on an irrational basis.

integrate: to open to people of all races, creeds or religion.

Ku Klux Klan: a secret society of whites created after the Civil War to intimidate African Americans.

lynch: to execute without due process of law, often by means of hanging.

NAACP: National Association for the Advancement of Colored People, an organization created in 1909 to fight discrimination against African Americans.

plaintiff: a person who sues in court.

poll tax: a tax imposed on the right to vote; prohibited in national elections by the Civil Rights Act of 1964.

primary: an election in which registered members of a political party choose candidates to run for office.

rebut: to present opposing arguments.

segregate: to isolate a person or group of people.

solicitor general: chief lawyer for the government.

sue: a legal term meaning to accuse a person of wrongdoing in a civil court.

Supreme Court: highest federal court in the United States, consists of nine justices appointed by the President and approved by the Senate.

unanimous: without difference of opinion.

v, v.: against, used in titles of court cases.

verdict: decision of a jury or judge.

Notes

CHAPTER 1 NOTES
p.9 "Nigga, don't you never push ..." Fenderson, Lewis. *Thurgood Marshall: Fighter for Justice*, p.11
p.9 "Break it up!" ... Fenderson, op.cit. p.11
p.10 "When I saw what you did ..." *New York Post*, June 14, 1960
p.10 "If anybody calls you Nigger, ..." James Haskins, *Thurgood Marshall*, p.11
p.10 "I got tired of spelling ..." Michael Davis and Hunter Clark, *Thurgood Marshall: Warrior at the Bar, Rebel on the Bench*, p.31
p.10 "We lived on a respectable street ..." Davis & Clark, op.cit., p. 37
p.12 "The truth is you learn ..." Roger Goldman with David Gallen, *Thurgood Marshall: Justice for All*, p.144
p.12 "I can still see him ...." Richard Kluger, *Simple Justice*, p.173
p.12 "He never told me ..." *Newsweek*, June 26, 1967
p.13 "My dad, my brother, and I ..." Ed Edwin tapes in the Columbia Oral History Collection, Columbia University, 1977, p.5
p.13 "I am with your parents ..." Davis & Clark, op.cit., p.39
p.14 "Before I left that school ..." Davis & Clark, op.cit., p.37
p.15 "His more polite descendants like ..." Kluger, op.cit., p.173
p.16 "Finally Grandma Annie emerged ... Kluger, op. cit., p.174
p.16 "Boy, we can get a man ..." Kluger, op. cit., p.323

CHAPTER 2 NOTES
p.19 "At one point ..." Carl Rowan, *Dream Makers, Dream Breakers*, 1993
p.19 "If I were taking ..." Davis & Clark, op.cit. p.46

p.20 "You had to do something ..." Haskins, op.cit., p.23
p.21 "Nigger, why don't you ..." Fenderson, op.cit., p.38
p.21 "We found out that ..." Davis & Clark, op.cit., p.45
p.22 "I guess that's ..." Davis & Clark, op.cit. p.45
p.22 "At times, ..." Rowan, op.cit., p.44
p.22 "We went there because ..." Davis & Clark, op.cit.   p.49
p.22 "You were so busy ..." Rowan, op.cit., p.151
p.23 "Thurgood, you are a disgrace ... any time you wanna ..." Davis & Clark, op.cit., p.42
p.24 "This is what I wanted ..." Davis & Clark, op.cit., p.48
p.25 "What Charlie beat into our heads ..." Davis & Clark, op.cit., p.55
p.25 "When I was in law school ..." Goldman & Gallen, op.cit., p.145

CHAPTER THREE NOTES
p.31 "I bought some ... the phone company would call ..." Rowan, op.cit., p.70
p.32 "It was all part ..." Davis & Clark, op.cit., p.134
p.32 "I will not be ..." Ed Edwin, op.cit., p.88
p.34 "We're in the education business ..." Fenderson, op.cit., p.74
p.34 "It was sweet revenge ..." Davis & Clark, op.cit., p.90
p.34 "When the time of execution ..." Davis & Clark, op.cit., p.320
p.34 "Personally I would not give up ..." Haskins, op.cit., p.47
p.35 "Thurgood Marshall was *of* the people ..." Kluger, op.cit., p.222
p.36 "I whooped and hollered ..." Rowan, op.cit., p.70
p.36 "How very tush-tush ..." Haskins, op.cit., p.47
p.36 "Charlie would sit ..." Haskins, op.cit.,p.47
p.38 "When I came home ..." Haskins, op.cit., p.50
p.38 "From now on ..." Fenderson, op.cit., p.81
p.39 "The chief of police told ... and when he saw me ..." Davis & Clark, op.cit.,p.106
p.39 " ...we had to keep dodging ..." Kluger, op.cit., p.225

CHAPTER 4 NOTES
p.41 "We get either a letter ..." Davis & Clark, op.cit., p.110
p.41 "...deep and real affection ..." Kluger, op.cit., p.326
p.42 "I ain't scared... during that first night..." Rowan, op.cit., p.107
p.42 "The whole damn court system ..." Rowan, op.cit., p.98
p.44 "Use this to buy ..." Rowan, op.cit., p.97

p.44 "... for no real reason ... the poor, the ignorant ... " Goldman & Gallen, op.cit., p.213

p.44 "It's the old story ..." Rowan, op.cit., p.386

p.44 "I think the people ..." Rowan, op.cit.,p.102

p.45 "... this white man came up ..." Goldman & Gallen, op.cit., p.148

p.45 "I think she took it ...I go into these ..." Rowan, op.cit., p.113

p.46 "No matter how much education ..." Rowan, op.cit., p.80

p.46 "The responsibility for enforcement ..." Rowan, op.cit., p.126

p.48 "He wore natty ..." Haskins, op.cit., p.50

p.48 "Hell, I'm not burr-headed ..." Rowan, op.cit., p.115

p.48 "I ride in the for-colored-only cabs ..." Kluger, op.cit., p.324

p.48 "I couldn't believe ..." Rowan, op.cit., p.103

p.49 "The only way to get equality ..." Rowan, op.cit., p.152

p.49 "They [the police] destroyed the Negro community ..." *New York Times*, June 9, 1946

p.50 "Then I heard a voice ..." Rowan, op.cit., p.108

p.50 "I'm not going ... The magistrate turned ..." Rowan, op.cit., p.109

CHAPTER FIVE NOTES

p.54 "Those racial supremacy boys ..." Goldman & Gallen, op.cit., p.92

p.55 "... Mr. Civil Rights ... the nation's biggest race man ..." Davis & Clark, op.cit., p.121

p.55 "You had yours ..." Goldman & Gallen, op.cit., p.149

p.55 "The broadest shoulders of all ..." Haskins, op.cit., p.76

p.55 "He's nervous now ..." Kluger, op. cit., p.561

p.55 "The only reason I look good ..." Davis & Clark, op.cit., p.21

p.56 "Thurgood was a good poker player ..." Davis & Clark, op.cit., p.133

p.56 "I despise nigger troops ..." Davis & Clark, op.cit,.p.130

p.57 "Don't you tell me ... that's when he said ..." Davis & Clark, op.cit., p.128

p.58 "I told the staff ..." Kluger, op. cit., p.316

p.58 "... would pose a question ..." Kluger, op. cit., p.338

p.59 "I slammed that *News and Courier* ..." Rowan, op.cit., p.20

p.59 "You know, Kenneth,..." Kluger, op. cit., p.324

CHAPTER 6 NOTES

p.61 "Don't worry, darling ..." Kluger, op. cit., p.561

p.61 "If you show ..." Davis & Clark, op.cit., p.154

p.63 "... the plain purpose ..." Rowan, op.cit., p.4

p.63 "...in the South, ..." Davis & Clark, op.cit., p.165

p.63 "We shall get a finer balance, ..." Rowan, op.cit., p.200

p.63 "Segregation of Negroes ..." Goldman & Gallen, op.cit., p.98

p.64 "My heart dropped ..." Rowan, op.cit., p.203

p.64 "... there can be no doubt ..." Goldman & Gallen,   op.cit., p.103

p.64 "Yeah, page five ..." Kluger, op. cit., p.642

p.65 "I have *never* seen a man ..." Kluger, op. cit., p. 636

p.65 "We'll have no ..." Kluger, op. cit., p.642

p.65 "What do you want ..." Kluger, op. cit., p.643

p.65 "... when we niggers ..." Kluger, op. cit., p.643

p.66 "Everybody knows that ..." Kluger, op. cit., p. 674

p.68 "... we believe ..." Goldman & Gallen, op.cit., p.106

p.68 "We hit the jackpot!" Rowan, op.cit., p.218

p.68 "That was when ..." Edwin, op.cit., p.99

p.69 "I thought the world ..." Davis & Clark, op.cit., p.180

p.69 "Put the dumb colored children ..." Kluger, op. cit.,   p.730

p.70 "It is interesting to me ..." Kluger, op. cit., p.735

p.70 "We're gonna be back ..." Haskins, op.cit., p.98

p.70 "... but we shall not negotiate ..." Davis & Clark, op.cit., p.183

p.71 "Law can change things ..." Goldman & Gallen, op.cit.,   p.112

p.71 "We shall resort ..." Davis & Clark, op.cit., p.183

p.71 "Heaven knows ..." Davis & Clark, op.cit., p.181

p.71 "I have always been in favor ..." Rowan, op.cit., p.387

CHAPTER SEVEN NOTES

p.73 "We've got the law, religion, and God ..." Rowan, op.cit., p.281

p.73 "... difficult if not impossible for any Negro ..." Davis & Clark, op.cit., p.185

p.74 "Even if it be claimed ..." Davis & Clark, op.cit., p.194

p.74 "It would take two ..." Haskins, op.cit., p.107

p.74 "They don't mean go slow ..." Haskins, op.cit., p.107

p.76 "I'd give 'em the same ..." *Newsweek*, July 8, 1991

p.76 "Police wouldn't let me ..." Edwin, op.cit., p.61

p.77 "... when one has the opportunity ..." Davis & Clark, op.cit., p.13

p.78 "Tell your brother ..." Davis & Clark, op.cit., p.236

p.78 "They don't really hate me ..." Haskins, op.cit., p.112

p.78 " ... I guess the answer is ..." Edwin, op.cit., p.

p.78 "I enjoy the slower pace ..." Fenderson, op.cit., p.111

p.81 "I told Cissy that ..." Davis & Clark, op.cit., p.245
p.81 "I accepted because the President ..." Haskins, op.cit., p.124
p.81 "Once in a while, I'll catch ..." Davis & Clark, op.cit., p.252
p.82 "... our nation has progressed ..." Rowan, op.cit., p.290
p.82 "Hell, I ain't ..." Davis & Clark, op.cit., p.255
p.84 "I volunteered ..." Rowan, op.cit., p.295
CHAPTER EIGHT NOTES
p.85 "Nothing will be settled ..." Rowan, op.cit., p.433
p.85 "I resented that crap ..." Rowan, op.cit., p.365
p.86 "... all they would have heard ..." Davis & Clark, op.cit. p.261
p.86 "I'm going to put ..." Edwin, op.cit., p.108
p.86 "I believe it is ..." *Newsweek*, June 26, 1967
p.88 "I'm thinking about a widow ..." Fenderson, op.cit., p.126
p.89 "That was a fun assignment ..." Rowan, op.cit., p.341
p.89 "If the First Amendment ..." Goldman & Gallen, op.cit., p.16
p.89 "What I want to talk to you ..." Davis & Clark, op.cit., p.288
p.90 "I don't believe that ..." Rowan, op.cit.,p.360
p.90 "It's a private matter ..." Davis & Clark, op.cit., p.292
p.92 "What's shakin' ..." Davis & Clark, op.cit., p.303
p.92 "When school boards fail ..." Davis & Clark, op.cit., p.308
p.92 "It may be easy ..." Davis & Clark, op.cit., p.316
p.93 "When young lawyers apply ..." Rowan, op.cit., p.347
p.93 "Nearly half of the clerks ..." Goldman & Gallen, op.cit., p.177
CHAPTER NINE NOTES
p.94 "When the prison gates ..." Rowan, op.cit., p.383
p.95 "Unless our children ..." Kluger, op. cit., p.773
p.95 "After 20 years, ..." Wilkinson, J. Harvie. *From Brown to Bakke*,
p.225
P.95 "Dunno, but more than ..." Rowan, op.cit., p.328
P.95 "Over 200 years, ..." Goldman & Gallen, op.cit., p.18
p.96 "I just want to be sure ..." Sunstein, Cass. *Stanford Law Review*,
Summer 1992, p.1275
p.96 "The dream of America ..." Goldman & Gallen, op.cit., p.261
p.97 "I didn't give advice ..." Davis & Clark, op.cit., p.299
p.97 "If you are going to do ..." Goldman & Gallen, op.cit., p.175
p.98 "They need to stop ..." Goldman & Gallen, op.cit., p.156
p.98 "The trouble is ..." Rowan, op.cit., p.388

p.98 "If I die, ..." *Time,* July 8, 1991

p.99 "This scheme forces ..." Goldman & Gallen, op.cit., p.241

p.100 "I think the next justice ..." *Ebony,* May 1990

p.100 "You know what worries me ..." *Ebony,* May 1990

p.100 "I'm still kickin' ...." Rowan, op.cit., p.411

p.101 "How do you feel ..." Davis & Clark, op.cit., p.4-6

p.102 "He did the best ..." Rowan, op.cit., p.392

p.103 "If we stop now ..." Haskins, op.cit., p.98

BIBLIOGRAPHY

Branch, Taylor. *Parting the Waters: America in the King Years, 1954-63*. New York: Simon and Schuster, 1988.

Commission on the Bicentennial of the United States Constitution. *The Supreme Court of the United States*. 1992.

Davis, Michael and Hunter Clark. *Thurgood Marshall: Warrior at the Bar, Rebel on the Bench*. New York: Birch Lane Press, 1992.

Edwin, Ed. Columbia University Oral History Research Office, 1977.

Fenderson, Lewis. *Thurgood Marshall: Fighter for Justice*. New York: McGraw-Hill Book Company, 1969.

Goldman, Roger and David Gallen. *Thurgood Marshall: Justice for All*. New York: Carroll & Graf, 1992.

Haskins, James. *Thurgood Marshall: A Life for Justice*. New York: Henry Holt and Co., 1992.

Kluger, Richard. *Simple Justice*. New York: Vintage Books, 1977.

Rowan, Carl T. *Dream Makers, Dream Breakers*. Boston: Little, Brown and Co., 1993.

Scwartz, Bernard. *Super Chief: Earl Warren and his Supreme Court—A Judicial Biography*. New York: New York University Press, 1983.

Wilkinson, J. Harvie. *From Brown to Bakke*. New York: Oxford University Press, 1979.

Woodward, Bob and Scott Armstrong. *The Brethren*. New York: Avon, 1979.

INDEX